CW00970723

How to use this guide

For restaurants, the new venues come first, then establishments are alphabetical within cuisine type. After the new venues in bars, the section is alphabetical. Pubs are alphabetical within geographical areas.

A map of the city centre can be found at the back of this book. Central Manchester map references are given after telephone numbers and are in red.

Upon publication, this guide was as up to date as we could make it, but please call ahead to check opening times etc. Circumstances in catering change rapidly.

Editor and principal writer:
Jonathan Schofield (0161 211 2716)
jonathan.schofield@citylife.co.uk

Writers and researchers:
David Lloyd, Ruth Allan, Neil Porter, Emma Unsworth, Jon-Paul Waddington, Lianne Steinberg, Richard Hector-Jones, Marissa Burgess, Emma Barnett, Jay Barnett, Diana Carthy, John Clarke, Philip Hamer, Thom Hetherington, Jo Elliott-Mell, Vicki Holman, Vanessa Lees, Sara Newman, Sharon McCarthy, Jacob, Oliver and Ralph Schofield

Art director: Nick Cooper (0161 211 2280)

Designers: Marcus Graham, Emma Williams

Illustrator: Kelly Dyson

Cover picture: Market Restaurant

Distribution: Tim Woosey (0161 211 2633), Michael Scurfield

Marketing: Rachel Spiller

Advertising: Gemma Minshull, Vanessa Doeg

Publisher: Jacqui Pacey

Published by Diverse Media Ltd, 164 Deansgate, Manchester M3 3RN. Part of Guardian Media Group.

Co1

Introduction

Flying rats are horrible, but tender little squab pigeons cooked and exquisitely presented at the River Restaurant by Eyck Zimmer are easier to love. You can get similarly affectionate about the generous bellies of pigs glazed with honey and found on a bed of puy lentils under the supervision of Kai Smith at Mr Thomas's Chop House. Nor is it easy to ignore the enticing aromas of sizzling meatloaf floating from the giant pan in Katsouris on John Dalton Street.

Just as with 2004, the last 12 months have delivered sublime food and drink experiences. But it's been very different than last year. There have been few big restaurant openings, for instance. Just as well given that several of the 2004 arrivals have struggled. Fine dining ventures such as Establishment and the Cotton House for one reason or another haven't had quite the impact they should. In the end, it was the blindside arrival at the River Restaurant of Eyck Zimmer and his deceptively simple cooking that brought fresh excitement to city centre tastebuds. Similarly EastZEast in Princess Street brought new stumulus to Indian cuisine.

Other advances in subcontinental food took place further afield with Dilli and Saffron Lounge in Altrincham and Hale respectively. Meanwhile 2005 saw the consolidation of a southern crescent of suburban over-achievement from Urmston to Didsbury, with small, proprietor-run establishments such as Isinglass, Fat Loaf, Marmalade, Rhubarb and Café Jem&I.

Back in the city centre, a welcome return was made by the Crown and Kettle in Great Ancoats Street, a pub with one of the most startling ceilings in the country, although management plans to put a TV in every room are misguided. Every year, beer provision gets better too - Greater Manchester can heartily raise a glass to itself. According to the latest CAMRA *Good Beer Guide* we have 23 independent brewers - London only has 10 and Merseyside 5.

The Crown and Kettle lies in the Northern Quarter of the city centre and this is where many of the good new bars have arrived, such as the suitably quirky Odd and the weirdly functional Common. The rise and rise of this most interesting, down-at-heel yet upbeat, decayed yet developing area continues to delight. In time, and with care - you listening there, Council? - we could have a real city quarter that is pure

on Livebait, but it could be many others. They have a Thai fish curry - why not just a fish curry? In a city with 30 different cuisines to choose from, restaurants shouldn't try to bamboozle people with maverick dish descriptions.

There's also a creeping tendency for service charges to appear on restaurant bills. At least OpusOne at the Radisson Edwardian has started to see sense, lowering their service charge from an insulting 12.5% to a merely annoying 10%. In this guide, we've highlighted establishments that apply service charges.

That's one of several changes in this edition of the guidebook. The most obvious alteration has been in the pubs section, where the city centre hostelries have been arranged into three pub crawls or picked out as food places. Please note, as well, that pubs and bars will have new licenses in place by November and that their opening hours may change.

We hope you enjoy this book and take as much pleasure in dining and drinking in Greater Manchester as our cartoon guest (left) does. Despite occasional inconsistencies and dud experiences, we are still spoilt by the variety and amount of good food and drink available.

There's always something fresh going on too. Big openings hit town once more with Cocoa Rooms and Room, both multi-functional restaurants and bars arrving in winter 2005. We'll see how they get on. It's the job of this book to keep you informed and help you find new favourites or rediscover old ones.

Manchester. Not a clone of districts in other cities, a tourist daydream or a single interest one-trick pony, but something that satisfies a broad range of locals and visitors through its individuality. On page 96, we celebrate High Street in the Northern Quarter. It's no coincidence that both the Restaurant and the Bar of the Year are located here - in the form of the wonderful 25-year-old Market Restaurant and the sassy Bluu - and that many of the nominees for awards came from the wonky grid of streets nearby.

Problems remain. Service hasn't improved much, but that's not just a Mancunian or even a British problem.

It'd be pleasant, too, if chefs could stop using inappropriate words in menus, particularly four-letter words such as Thai - although wild references to other national cuisines, presumably those that the chef hopes we aren't too familiar with, are just as irritating. Let's pick

Jonathan Schofield - Editor

Pricing and grading

Each restaurant is coded:

£A - £40 plus per person

£B - £15-£40 per person

£C - up to £15

These are guidelines only - prices might change, special offers might be posted. Please phone ahead if you wish to confirm prices. All establishments are licensed unless otherwise stated.

Establishments have been asked to supply details with regard to entertainment, children, vegetarian options, disabled access, set menus. If these details are omitted under the entries, it means that there are no such facilities and options or that the venue has failed to supply them. Disabled access information is supplied by the venue not through independent audit.

Individual dishes are distinguished by a capital letter on the first word of the description thus Grilled seabass etc… The dishes quoted are intended to help illustrate the type of food available and price range: these options may not still be available or the menu may have changed.

On your marks

Throughout this section, we judge restaurants out of five. Of course venues of poor quality are not considered for entry here, so marks will tend to be in the range of three and above. Please note that there has to be a degree of flexibility - venues can only be measured acording to their merits within their type of category. Thus a pizzeria is judged out of five with regard to other pizzerias, a Michelin star chasing restaurant is judged against those nationally who have already got a star.

Food quality: rated on the qualities of preparation, presentation, taste and value. Full marks of five would mean that repeat visits maintain the highest of standards.

Service: we judge this on the efficiency and the attentiveness of the service. But for five, there would have to be warmth too, an amiability that knows where to the draw the line before it becomes obtrusive.

Décor - again the first measure is whether the décor is appropriate for the venue, but places can also be marked highly for individual qualities such as their magnificence or eccentricity.

Restaurants

Azzurro £C

Burton Road, West Didsbury

0161 448 0099

Tue-Thu 5pm-11pm; Thu-Sat noon-2pm, 5pm-11pm

To the crowded Burton Road food scene comes Azzurro, a small independent venture serving modern Italian cuisine. The key quality here is good food, served by people who know and plainly love their menu. The main thing in short supply is space, so get there early to secure a table on weekends. There is a selection of ten or so market-fresh fish specials offered, such as Grilled sardines (£4.50) that intelligently swim the line between succulent insides and crisp-skinned exteriors. You might also go for the Involtini di melanzane (£4.95), griddled aubergine wrapped around a ricotta, pine nut and basil filling, served on a bed of deep-fried spaghetti. Mains such as Agnello marinato (£10.95), marinated and grilled leg of lamb steaks served on a spinach and mint pesto, with rosemary and garlic, are worth digging into as well.

Food 3.5 Service 4 Décor 2.5

Entertainment: occasional events
Children: several options
Vegetarian: various
Disabled access: partial

The Bakery £B

Heaton Moor Road, Heaton Moor

0161 432 2374

Daily 9am-11pm/midnight for drinks

As we all know, you need more than just the ingredients to make a good loaf rise. This is a worthy arrival to the Heatons, but its full potential has yet to be realised. Downstairs, the Bakery is marble-lined and minimal, filled with premium vodkas, cherry wood tables and black-shirted, handsome waiters. Groups of Heatonites chat amiably with a KFC soundtrack filling in the blanks. Upstairs, the restaurant is more simple - almost like a suburban outpost of a middle-market chain. The food's fine. You might want to try starters of Pan fried halloumi with rocket salad and tomato confit (£4.95), or Asparagus, roasted peppers and goats cheese (£5.95) and mains such as the Cumbrian fillet of beef with cheese potato cake and wilted spinach (£15.95) or Marinated Thai monkfish with spiced sweet potatoes and Thai coconut sauce (£12.95), which create good flavours.

Food 3 Service 3.5 Décor 2

Entertainment: occasional events
Children: separate menu
Vegetarian: various options
Set menu: between 5pm-7pm, two courses for £14.95

Bawadi Café £C

Cheetham Hill Road, Cheetham Hill

0161 832 2345

Daily 11am-11pm

If certain locations have a historical predestination, Cheetham Hill and Red Bank's is immigration. For 150 years, successive waves of new arrivals have washed up on the western bank of the River Irk. Now we've got a Lebanese café-cum-restaurant that also does Med staples such as pizzas and pasta. The interior of this former early 19th century residence has been brought back to its original size by removing the false ceilings and showing off the lovely cornice. Complete with shisha pipe - for use, not just decoration - plus exposed bricks and two big timber tables, this is a great little space. The winning dish on the *City Life* visit was the Kafta meshwi (£5.50), lamb ground up and then mixed with spices and so on, with heat coming from sweet green peppers. And the banana milkshake (£1.85) is worth the short hop from town.

Food 3.5 Service 4 Décor 4

Entertainment: the shisha pipe
Children: various from main menu
Vegetarian: several dishes
Set menu: various deals

Slip off Albert Square, onto Princess Street, into Crisp Restaurant. The warm welcome from owners and staff tells you this is no chain restaurant, and the friendly, relaxed atmosphere complements the colourful, modern interior and cosy cellar bar perfectly.

The menu is superb! Italian cuisine with a twist! Creamy goats cheese and mango chutney on a bed of rocket, a treat to say the least, followed by seabass fillet - cooked to perfection. Traditional Italian Salva for dessert (chocaholic heaven) and rich, fragrant Lavazza expresso, the finishing touch to a top notch dining experience for any age or occasion.

Fresh produce, homemade dishes and fast & friendly service make Crisp the ideal choice for a quick bite with friends or a romantic meal for two.

R E S T A U R A N T
PIZZA, PASTA, GRILL & SALAD

FREE
glass of house wine for all City Life readers having a starter & main course
(quote City Life or bring in this voucher for free wine)

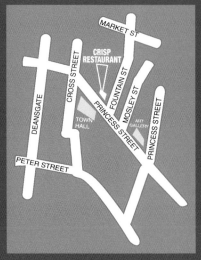

63 PRINCESS STREET, MANCHESTER
TEL: 0161 244 5858
www.crisp-restaurant.com
Open 7 days: 11am - 11pm
IDEAL FOR MEALS BEFORE OR AFTER THE SHOW

The Glass House at Broomstairs
£B/C

Hyde Road, Denton

0161 320 1101

Mon-Sat noon-11pm; Sun noon-10.30pm

This is one of those 'interesting' places that have obviously seen plenty of life, so it's a bit worn about the edges. But food wise, the Glass House does the simple things right. It's run by the people behind the Three Arrows close to Heaton Park - Sue and Stuart Norman. Good courses enjoyed by *City Life* include homemade Steak and kidney pudding (£7.95), served with a powerful meat gravy, peas and a rich mash complete with a suet crust. The One pot (£7.95) was another British fave, this time beef braised in Mackeson stout with roasted root veg, new potatoes and a Stilton-infused pastry crust. If you're in the area, this is worth a try.

Food 3.5 Service 4 Décor 2

Entertainment: the punters
Children: welcome, variety of menu options
Vegetarian: several options
Disabled access: partial

The Cotton House
£A

Ducie Street, City

0161 237 5052 10E

www.thecottonhouse.net

Mon-Wed 7am-midnight; Thu-Fri 7am-2am; Sat 9am-2am; Sun breakfast only

Given its size, scale and ambition, the Cotton House should have rocked the world. But it's still not quite rocking Manchester. First off, you have to ask whether Piccadilly is the right location for this scale of venture. And the answer is no. Secondly, the place is very big. The dining space, part of the gargantuan ground floor of a railway warehouse from 1867, stretches into infinity whilst the bar merely overstretches the concept. Fortunately, there are some clever design touches here from Mueller and Kneer, especially the excellent waterfalls of filigree curtains separating diners. The food is the high point of any visit, but it can be inconsistent - as can the welcome from the staff. Sample dishes include Terrine of ham hock and parsley cornichons with Dijon dressing (£5) or Pan roasted Goosnargh chicken, fondant potato, green beans and jus gras (£15.50). Desserts are created with care and flair such as the Morello dark cheescake (£6), or the selection of homemade sorbets and Tulle biscuits (£6). To sum up, when the Cotton House gets the food right, it usually does a fine job and more than justifies the visit. But when it doesn't, that big space just seems even more cavernous.

Food 4 Service 3.5 Décor 4

Entertainment: DJs and occasional events
Children: options from the menu
Vegetarian: several options
Service charge: 10%
Set menu: offered
Disabled access: full

New Restaurants

Dilli £A/B

60 Stamford New Road, Altrincham

0161 927 9219

www.dilli.co.uk

Mon-Sun noon-11pm

Dilli is ambitious, calling itself 'the real taste of India' and promising customers the best Indian food in the North. After an opening few weeks when it struggled to be the best food in Altrincham, it's beginning to live up to this immodest claim. Sharp to look at with a crisp and clean interior adorned with wood carvings and sparkling glasses, silver cutlery and swish crockery, you can now immediately spot that this place takes pride in itself. The food described as 'vintage Indian cuisine' is under the guidance of Kuldeep Singh, apparently one of the top ten Indian chefs in the UK, and Raminder Pal Singh Malhotra, an expert in ayurvedic cooking. On the menu there isn't a chicken

korma in sight, with a tempting array of different dishes instead, all guaranteeing fresh ingredients prepared the traditional way. From the array of flavour on offer, perhaps try starters of Calamari peri peri (£6.45) chewy curls of squid delicately tumbled with curry leaves, mustard and pepper, or the delicate Shikhampuri kebab (£3.95), baby lamb cooked with cinnamon and yoghurt cheese (£3.95). Mains might include Jhinga hara pyaz (£11.95), fat, juicy prawns stir-fried with spring onions or Methi murgh (£8.95), hunks of chicken wrapped in a squeakily fresh tumble of spinach and fenugreek.

Food 4 Service 4 Décor 4

Entertainment: comprehensive events programme
Children: very welcome, many choices from the menu
Vegetarian: many options
Service charge: 12.5%
Set menu: several
Disabled access: full

The Cedar Tree £B

17 Huddersfield Road, Newhey, Rochdale

01706 842 626

Wed-Fri noon-2pm; Tue-Fri 6.30pm-9.30pm; Sat 7pm-9.30pm

The Cedar Tree is understated in its ambience and more akin to a cosy tearoom than a faux French gaff with clichéd Parisian murals. It makes for a great escape out of the city centre and into the surrounding uplands, whether by car (exit 21, M63) or train. There is a short but varied à la carte menu with stand-outs such as the evocative Lancashire grill consisting of black pudding, field mushroom, smoked bacon and Lancashire cheese with a warm mustard sauce (£5.50). The Summer Bistro Menu offers three courses for £14.95, except on weekends when it rises to £17.95. Whatever you eat, leave room for the puddings - the crumble, containing a fruity cocktail of apple, mango and banana, remains long in the memory.

Food 4 Service 4 Décor 3

Entertainment: gourmet evening every last Fri of the month (£29.95 per person)
Children: smaller portions
Vegetarian: 3 starters, 1 main
Set menu: early bird menu, 2 courses for £10, 6.30pm-7.30pm on week nights, 2 course lunch special for £5
Disabled access: full

ƎSTABLISHMƎNT

43-45 Spring Gardens,
Manchester M2 2BG
0161 839 6300
www.establishmentrestaurant.com

Egon Ronay starred

4* *(Ray King, Manchester
Evening News, May 2004)*

Nominee - Newcomer of the
year - *City Life 2004*

4/5 Food - City Life 2004

Nominee - Best Wine List
- *City Life 2004 and 2005*

Best Restaurant Award
- *Hi Life Platinum 2005*

New Restaurants

EastZEast £B

Ibis Hotel, Princess Street,
City
0161 244 5353
www.eastzeast.com 8G
**Sun-Thu 5pm-midnight; Fri-Sat
5pm-1am**

Sometimes prejudices about restaurants connected to budget hotels are reliable. Sometimes, you have to be prepared to be proven completely wrong. And the latter is the case with EastZEast, a new, and almost unpronounceable, Punjabi restaurant that has opened underneath the Ibis Hotel on Princess Street. This is something for the curry connoisseur - only Shimla Pinks offers a cut above in central Manchester at the moment. Rusholme has almost become a poor chilli fans' Vegas, its neon lights and fast food attitude barely changing from restaurant to restaurant along the strip. It's a place for clubbers and footie fans to mop up the night's excesses.

Not so at EastZEast. The concept is to provide a place to wake up or wind down rather than just nod off. Brown leather chairs and slick black tables are brightened with colourful spotlights and a floor-to-ceiling waterfall encased in glass panels. Great food comes in the form of Aloo paratha (£2.75), a deceptively dry looking chapatti filled with moist mashed potatoes and fresh coriander, the Prawn fry (£4.95), tiger prawns shallow fried and served with an impressive garnish of peppery leaves, the Karahi bhindi gosht (£8.95), lamb cooked with okra, and Karahi paneer shahi (£8.50), cheese with tomatoes, mustard seeds and cream of cashew nuts.

Food 4.5 Service 5 Décor 4

Entertainment: occasional
Children: very welcome, many choices from the menu
Vegetarian: many options
Set menu: several
Disabled access: full

Dr Livvy's £C/B

High Street, City
0161 839 2109 7C
**Mon-Sat noon-midnight; Sun
noon-11pm**

Although professing to be largely dedicated to Afro-Caribbean cuisine, the restaurant-bar, now filling the space once occupied by popular tramp stop the Blob Shop, serves up spicy food from all over the world - or 'the world' as defined by decent pub grub, at any rate. As well having a comfortable, booth-lined dining area, Dr Livvy's has become an atmospheric bar kitted out with colonial-style ceiling fans and warm orange lighting. Forget the jacket spuds and Thai fish cakes and head for the Carribbean, with dishes such as Ackee and salt fish (£3.70) or the fun-sounding Doc's prescription (£9.90), a mixed platter of curried patti, jerk chicken, plantain, Jamaican dumpling, rice and peas. Advice here though: swap the patti for a small serving of blue mountain curried lamb, which is rich and delicious.

Food 3 Service 3.5 Décor 4

Entertainment: comprehensive events programme
Children: welcome, several choices from the menu
Vegetarian: limited
Disabled access: full

Fat Loaf £B

62 Green Lane, Aston-on-Mersey, Sale

0161 972 0397

Tue-Sat 5.30pm-10pm

The modest façade doesn't make this place easy to find, but the décor inside is soothingly simple. Wooden furniture and slate floor tiles are warmed by neon artwork. Starters range from Soda bread with home made chutney and brie (£4.50) to Crab linguine with chilli, lime and parsley (£5.80). Chunky fillets of mackerel (£10.50) give a meaty weight to the parma ham, mozzarella and tomato salad. Fat Loaf's owners are Paul Taylor and Timothy Wood, who discovered a shared love of good food whilst working in the kitchens of the Lowry and Malmaison in the city. This venture is a credit too them, a homely type of affair and a model of good service. Fat Loaf is recommended for down to earth food lovers.

Food 4 Service 5 Décor 3

Children: welcome, smaller portions available

Vegetarian: variety of starters and mains

Set menus: Wed-Fri 5.30pm-6.45pm, 2 courses and coffee £12.50

Disabled access: partial

The Greyhound £B

Church Road, Urmston

0161 748 2063

www.thegreyhoundflixton.co.uk

Mon-Sat noon-3pm, 5.30pm-late; Sun noon-late

This former Beefeater pub has been taken over by city chef Robert Owen Brown, 2004's Food and Drink Festival Chef of the Year. And there's a lot of Beefeater left yet in his new gaff, as the refurb remains minimal. Service is excellent, however, and the food shows hallmark Owen Brown strengths of simplicity and clever thinking. Try fish dishes such as the Roast salmon fillet with Morecambe bay shrimps and cockles (£8.95) or Monkfish roasted with fondant potatoes, wilted greens and a fennel jus (£14.95). Meat dishes such as Welsh rack of lamb with apricots in a puff pastry case on creamy mash with a lamb jus (£13.50) are equally good. Urmston might not be the new Bray, but with its not-too-distant neighbour Isinglass and now the confident Greyhound, it's definitely on the up.

Food 3.5 Service 4 Décor 2.5

Children: children's portions

Vegetarian: 2 starters, 1 main, other vegetarian orders on request

Hanaan £B

Princess Street, City

0161 228 7675 7F

Mon-Thu noon-2.30pm, 5pm-midnight; Fri noon-2.30pm, 5pm-3am; Sat noon-3am; Sun noon-11pm

Hanaan first opened in Rusholme over a decade ago and was one of the original sub-continental restaurants that moved away from nursing-home carpet and flock wallpaper. Its new place is another lesson in how a contemporary Indian restaurant can look. You might want to try the dining deal with three mix-and-match set menus for £7, such as the Chicken pakora, the Balti lamb and basmati rice followed by ice cream. The best part of this is the lamb, a blend of lean meat, with herbs and spices in a thick sauce. The taste bud titillation here is provided by the coriander, which links hands with the lamb and the other ingredients in an all-singing, all-dancing Bollywood number for the palate. Nearly as good was the Saag aloo (£4.20), a suitably biting and robust blend of potato and spinach with a hot kick.

Food 3 Service 4 Décor 3.5

Entertainment: occasional

Children: very welcome, many choices from the menu

Vegetarian: many options

Set menu: several

New Restaurants

Marmalade £B

60 Beech Road, Chorlton

0161 232 1273

Tue-Sat 11am-11pm; Sun 11am-10.30pm

Winner of *City Life* Manchester Food and Drink Festival Newcomer of the Year Award 2005. The plan here is for a good British alternative to the countless bistros and brasseries you bump into whilst tootling through France. Thus the food is robust, skilfully put together and North West sourced where available. What the restaurant is trying to do is shown by the Chicken thigh and breast (£10.95) - yes, a chicken dish that stands out! Entitled A bit of leg and a bit of breast (a disappointment for those who favour the arse), the fowl is corn fed and free range with pale yellow flesh packed with real flavour. The accompaniment is perfect - potatoes with mushrooms, peas, shallots and bacon plus some unexpected sun-blushed tomatoes. Don't miss the puddings. On first sight, the Strawberries with short bread biscuits and clotted cream (£4.50) look to have been ruined by extraneous and unadvertised sauces, but dip into it and you might end up licking the plate. Drinks include a superior wine list and even dandelion and burdock, sarsaparilla and ginger beer from Fitzpatrick's Herbal Health in Rawtenstall. This is a buzzy, neighbourhood restaurant and bar that is well-managed and has good service. Occasionally the presentation of the food needs improving, but otherwise this is very worthy winner of Newcomer of the Year.

Food 4 Service 4 Décor 3.5

Children: separate children's menu

Vegetarian: special plus 2 starters and 2 mains

Disabled access: full

The Lazy Toad £B

Ashton Hill Lane, Droylsden

0161 301 3031

Wed (tapas night) 5pm-9.30pm; Thu 5pm-9.30pm; Fri-Sat 5pm-10pm; Sun 1pm-7pm

In 2004, this Droylsden pub and restaurant picked up Tameside's Restaurant of the Year Award. It's certainly interesting, even curious. For instance, once through the pub the décor is clean and sharp, but with additions from regular customers of toad-related nick-nacks from around the world. The food is sort of Modern British meets Fusion meets whatever the chef feels, such as the decent Noisette of lamb on a bed of noodles with Thai sauce (£10.95). There are a few special effects too, such as the Frogs legs. The cooking can be clumsy, though, and the Lazy Toad might want to let the food breathe a little. On the upside, the owners are charming and atmosphere easy going and free of stress. Concentrate on these elements and the Lazy Toad leaps ahead of the competition.

Food 3 Service 4 Décor 3

Entertainment: occasional

Children: very welcome, many choices from the menu

Vegetarian: many options

Set menu: several

Disabled access: full

Lotus Bar and Dim Sum £B/C

35A King Street, City

0161 832 9724 5D

www.yang-sing.com

Mon-Sat 11am-11.30pm; Sun 11.30-9pm

Splendid offshoot of the Yang Sing restaurant, with an impressive red and black interior and an outside canopy (at the rear in St Ann's Yard) so large it could shelter the world population of chipmunks. The dim sum are as good as those in the famous parent restaurant and come at £1 a shot (minimum two pieces). The Cuttle fishcake with lime leaves is knockout, as are the Steamed beef dumplings. There's also an à la carte menu, plus rice and noodle dishes. Real winners are the Oriental lunch boxes (£6.90 meat, mixed, vegetarian, £7.50 seafood) presented in handsome lacquered black and red boxes. The wine and cocktail list is worth close study. The roof garden for pre-booked groups is the best in the city. This venue is perfect for shoppers or as an evening rendezvous for those who like it sophisticated yet easy.

Food 4 Service 4 Décor 4

Children: very welcome, dim sum can be perfect for them
Vegetarian: more than 15 choices
Disabled access: partial

Panama Hatty's £B

Brown Street, City

0161 832 8688 6D

Daily noon to 9.30pm (last food orders)

Difficult location this. Previous incumbents Chez Gerard and Time lived very brief lives. The only survivor was wine bar Brahms and Liszt, which for many years in the '80s and the '90s entertained punters with gassy bottled beers, hen parties and a tiddly dancefloor - sort of a prototype Brannigans. Panama Hatty's, with a parent operation in the unlikely location of Spurstow in Cheshire, is trying to buck this sorry recent trend. The pick of the dishes on the *City Life* visit was the Jambalaya (£12.95), a rich mix of prawns, shrimps, mussels, chicken and chorizo that works well. This wasn't Michelin star stuff - it didn't parade in high heels along the frontiers of taste and flavour - but it was all right. For an informal night, perhaps with a gang of mates, this place is definitely worth a try.

Food 3.5 Service 4 Décor 4

Entertainment: occasional
Children: very welcome, many choices from the menu
Vegetarian: many options
Set menu: combos and other deals
Disabled access: full

Brasserie on Portland £B

Best Western Princess Hotel, Portland Street, City

0161 236 5122 7E

Daily 11.30am-3pm, 6pm-11pm

There's good food to be found here. The Poached pear, Stilton cream cheese and walnut salad (£4.95) followed by Smoked haddock risotto, soft poached egg, herb oil and parmesan (£12.95) make for two excellent courses. The risotto is a real hit, rich and ripe with the fish perfectly cooked and the rice wonderfully textured. The poached egg on the review visit broke under gentle pressure and had been timed to the second. Puddings such as Vanilla rice pudding with strawberry compote (£4) and Crème caramel with forest fruits (£4) both maintained the standards set thus far. The only major problem lies with the décor - the building might be grand but the paintwork comes courtesy of the hitherto little known Crown paint range of Can't Be Bothered colours.

Food 4 Service 4 Décor 3

Children: very welcome
Vegetarian: 2 or 3 options
Disabled access: full

New Restaurants

Northern Quarter Restaurant and Bar £B

108 High Street, City

0161 832 7115 8B

www.tnq.co.uk

Tue-Sat noon-11pm; Sun noon-4pm

Jobe Ferguson's new place in this manically developing area is the handsomest of the bunch. It's a former shop unit with big windows that allow people inside to people watch outside, whilst those outside can stare at those inside. The view across High Street to the former fish market and its elaborately carved façade is a real treat. Food comes via Hamid Maiden, who has trained in top eateries in Casablanca, Paris and London. Maiden serves up gutsy fresh food using prime local ingredients with added flavours of the Med and beyond. Excellent starters include Beef carpaccio with capers and dressed wild rocket (£6.25) and the Horseradish and sweetcorn potato cake with sour cream (£4.95), whilst standout mains include the Rib-eye steak served with chips and slow-roasted tomato and aioli (£12.50) or Monkfish tail with herb crushed new potatoes and bok choy with smoked haddock rillete (£13.25). Care is shown also with desserts such as Red wine poached pear with amaretto biscuit and cream chantilly (£4.50). With a good drinks range, including an interesting dessert wine choice, the Northern Quarter Restaurant and Bar makes for a quality but informal evening out. During summer, you can also enjoy a glass or two on the wide pavement over the road under the handsome façade mentioned above.

Food 4 Service 4 Décor 4.5

Children: 1 course, children's portions available

Vegetarian: starters and mains

Disabled access: partial

Oca £B

Waterside Arts Centre,
Waterside Plaza, Sale

0161 962 6666

Mon-Sat 11.30am-11.30pm; Sun noon-11pm

The Waterside Arts Centre offers a much-needed addition to the cultural life of Sale, and Oca does likewise for the town's food scene. On our visit, well-prepared examples from the extensive pizza menu included Salmone (£7.20) with salmon fillet, white wine sauce, lemon, parsley and grape chutney and Florentina (£6.20) with fresh spinach, free range egg, olives, mozzarella and tomato. The one dish that stood out was the Panzoti (£7.95), subtly flavoured smoked salmon black(!) triangle ravioli in a cheesy white wine sauce. The glass front of this pizza and pasta place lets the light flood in to the pale décor and allows for people-watching in the canalside square, as does the patio for fair-weather drinking and dining. The large booths and impressive cocktail list add to impression that Oca is ideal for a night out with friends or family.

Food 4 Service 4 Décor 4

Entertainment: Live music Wed

Children: welcome, £4.95 menu of pizza/pasts, drink and ice-cream

Vegetarian: 6 starters, 17 mains

Disabled access: full

New Restaurants

Sherpa £C

Mauldeth Road West, Withington

0161 448 2206

Mon-Sat 5.30pm-midnight; Sun 5.30pm-11.30pm

This Nepalese place is a good little find - courtesy of a *City Life* reader's recommendation. Not that it looks up to much on the outside, with its location on a dreary precinct amidst run-down shops. Inside, it's simple in the extreme - a cream room with eight tables and a corner bar. The service, led by Tulsi Man Maharjan, is warm and efficient, and the food offers excellent value. Strong dishes include the Haaku chuwala (£5.50), richly spiced barbecued lamb, Aloo taamaa (£4.50), a potent mix of potato, beans and tomatoes, and the lovely Kadi paneer (£3.95), cheese made on the premises with peppers, onions and tomatoes. A real curiosity is the Moma (£3): spiced steamed lamb dumplings that have a clear Chinese inspiration. Sherpa is also a take-away, with free delivery within three miles.

Food 3.5 Service 5 Décor 3

Children: very welcome
Vegetarian: several options
Disabled access: full

Sweet Mandarin £B/C

Design House, Copperas Street, City

0161 832 8848 8B

www.sweetmandarin.com

Mon-Sat noon-11pm; Sun 5pm-11pm

Sweet Mandarin is a PR babe's wet dream. If you can't sell this then you've got problems. The place is run by third-generation Chinese twins and their younger sister, all in their 20s, who also happen to be a qualified tax solicitor, a financier and an engineer. The décor is simple, colour added by downlighting in red and gold, furniture featuring a booth in beige leather and a couple of big red sofas. Food such as Crispy won tons (£4.50), Japanese king prawn tempura (£4), Salt and pepper ribs (£5.50), Mabel's (the sister's mum) claypot chicken (£7.50) and the sizzling Manchurian fillet of beef (£9.50) provide decent quality, reasonably priced fare. Customer service is exceptional for all age groups, including the youngest and the messiest.

Food 3.5 Service 5 Décor 4

Entertainment: comprehensive events programme
Children: very welcome
Vegetarian: several options
Set menu: several
Disabled access: full

Tonic £B

48 Beech Road, Chorlton

0161 862 9934

Mon-Thu noon-11pm; Fri-Sat noon-late

Tonic provides a bit of flair and simple, good cuisine. The relaxed atmosphere is complemented by a stylish décor and an impressive range of cocktails - at the bottom of the menu there's a request for customers to create their own drinks. Food is served to you whilst you relax on seats of white leather and take in the retro wallpaper adorned with oriental art. There is an option of a set lunch menu offering dishes such as Mussels in garlic and wine with accompaniment of thickly cut chips. Beyond the set dishes, there is an array of light bites and exotic mezzos consisting of falafel, hummus, cheeses and dried meats for the decent price of £9.95. Tonic is a fine place in which to relax with friends, enjoy fine food, funky backing beats and any drink you desire.

Food 3.5 Service 5 Décor 4

Vegetarian: 3 mains
Set menu: 1 course £5.95, 2 courses £8.95, 3 courses £10.95

Villagio £B

44 Canal Street, City
0161 244 5222 8F
Daily noon-11pm

Despite its challenging, shallow site, Italian Villagio feels spacious and open. A bank of recessed, colour-changing spots throw soft pools of light against the far wall, tables are generously spaced and the exposed bricks are as shiny and polished as the silverware. The food is confident and decent enough. Starters of Anti pasti mixto (£8.95 for two) offer a rich stew of flavours, tangy spiced meats, sweet chutneys and squeakily fresh salads. Mains present the usual Italian dilemma: yes, the pizzas are doubtless light, authentic and delicious, but they're still just pizzas. A good test of an Italian restaurant's mettle is the carne. Villagio doesn't disappoint. Steaks are timed to perfection - chargrilled on the outside, soft and moist within - and Petto di pollo alla grilla (£8.95) shows what little miracles can be performed when you treat simple ingredients with ingenuity and attention to detail.

Food 3.5 Service 3.5 Décor 3.5

Children: welcome
Vegetarian: 40% of menu
Set menus: express lunch menu £4.95.
Disabled access: full

Yorgio's £B

North Parade, Parsonage Gardens, City
0161 839 3198 4C
Daily 11am-11pm

Yorgio's provides food that is described as Mediterranean but is more specifically Greek. Among countless dishes, a mix of tapas style and traditional mains, there's hardly a bum note. Souvlakia (£12.45), a three-meat chargrilled kebab with rice, cous cous and salad, is good. The Keftedes (£4.95), lamb meat balls in tomato sauce, are fine. And so on. The Kotopoulo (£4.85), chicken in a broth of lemon, wine and herbs, was a pleasant surprise that faded a little, on our visit, as we waded through the dish - a tad too much lemon? The Greek hero of the hour was a very good Lagoto (£11.95), pork diced in a deep brown sauce of garlic, vinegar and tomatoes, and powered into repeat visit status by the winning addition of walnuts.

Food 3.5 Service 4 Décor 2.5

Entertainment: jazz on two Fridays in the month
Children: welcome, variety of options
Vegetarian: several options
Set menus: speciality platters for 2 (vegetarian platter £9.95, meat platter £11.95, seafood platter £12.95)

Wagamama £C/B

No. 1 Spinningfields Square, City
0161 833 9883 4D
www.spinningfields@ wagamama.com
Mon-Sat noon-11pm; Sun 12.30pm-10.30pm

The second Manchester branch, but this time on ground level. Wagamama's renowned reputation for dishing up wholesome meals, in record time, is continued here. The décor is cool, while the no-nonsense attitude of the staff means the service is brisk and you are never neglected. Virtually as soon as your order is placed, your food will be with you. For just over £10, a two-course meal can be enjoyed. Varieties of mouth-watering gyoza (dumplings) are a favoured starter whilst ramen (soup), noodle and rice based dishes make up the fine selection of mains. Not the place for a lengthy meal, but if you want a guaranteed, scrumptious, filling meal that won't break the bank, nor exceed half an hour, this chic chain will see you right.

Food 4 Service 4 Décor 3

Children: kids like several dishes such as the ramens
Disabled access: full

New Restaurants

ZenZero £B

202 Burton Road, West Didsbury

0161 434 2777

Having moved from town into the rich hinterland of West Didsbury, the cooking of director and exec chef Vinnie Young has grown stronger. The best dish on a *City Life* visit was the special of Seabass (£15.50), which was presented in fillets with king prawns and cherry tomatoes in red and white garlic sauce. This looked the part and gave a good mix of textures and flavours. Other elements were more hit and miss, but more of the former than the latter. For instance, the Agnello (£13), lamb cooked pink in a lush sauce and with a sturdy accompaniment of veg, was a winner too, as was the Choc fudge cake (£3.75). Set inside a rich red room with tacky prints inside extravagant frames, there's a clever design mind at work here too.

Food 4 Service 4 Décor 4

Children: flexible - smaller portions available

Vegetarian: various, but ask if you want something made up

Set menu: early bird menu 2/3 course £10.99/£12.99

Argentinian

Gaucho Bar and Grill £B

2a St Mary's Street, off Deansgate, City

0161 833 4333 5C

Mon-Thu noon-10.30pm; Fri-Sat noon-11pm; Sun noon-10.30pm

City Life doesn't usually find chains too appealing - applying common standards over several sites makes for predictability and blandness. But the Gaucho is different, ploughing a meat-rich and distinctive Argentinian furrow. The pokey entrance is the only disappointment, but don't worry: that soon opens out into one of the most spectacular restaurant interiors in the city centre, a former church hall in which you could fit a herd of beef cattle. It's a shame about the *Battleship Galactica* style air-conditioning system running across the place, but you can't have everything. There are fish dishes, salads and so forth but you should try the gloriously and lovingly cooked South American steaks, such as the majestic Bife de lomo (£24.95) for a majestic Desperate Dan sized 400g fillet - although there are much smaller options and other cuts for half the price. If you want to go really crazy, you might try the Lomito de cuadril at 950g (£38) - to share, of course, unless you're really hungry. A more distinctive speciality is perhaps the Churrasco daellma (£20), a marinated spiral cooked beef fillet. The wine range is excellent, covering 140 Argentina selections from vineyards as much as 3,000 metres above sea level.

Food 4 Service 4 Décor 4.5

Entertainment: occasional live bands on Thursdays, laid-back tunes from a DJ on Saturdays

Children: smaller portions can be requested

Vegetarian: starters and mains

Groups: up to 40

Set menu: noon-6pm, any 2 lunch menu dishes for £10, plus add an extra dish for £5 extra

Disabled access: full

Armenian

British - Modern British

Armenian Taverna £C

Albert Square, City

0161 834 9025 5D

Tue-Fri noon-2.30pm, 5.30pm-11.30pm; Sat 5.30pm-midnight; Sun 5.30pm-11.30pm

With three decades of earnest endeavour in the city, the Kalanyan family must be doing something right. What they aren't doing is refurbishing. The '70s décor is, being kind, charming, with a mural that needs to be listed and preserved by English Heritage as typical of the time. But it's the food (it bears a strong similarity to other Near Eastern cuisines, such as Turkish and Greek) quality that stands out. The best way to find this out for yourself is by getting stuck into the banquets (meat £15.50, vegetarian £13.75). Otherwise, tuck into one of the khorovdik or charcoal kebabs, with the pick perhaps being the Gaizag trout (£9.40) marinated in oil, lemon juices and spices and served with peyvaz (kebab sauce) and rice.

Food 3.5 Service 3.5 Décor 3

Children: half portions
Vegetarian: up to 12 dishes, see main entry
Set menu: see banquets above

Assembly £B

Lapwing Lane, West Didsbury

0161 445 3653

www.theassemblydidsbury.co.uk

Mon-Fri noon-10.30pm; Sat 10am-11pm; Sun 10am-10.30pm

Since changing from the Nose to the Assembly a couple of years ago, this good-looking venue has gone from strength to strength, and it more than repays a visit. With easy-going, excellent food in a comfortable atmosphere, given extra zest by the buzz of conversation, it's one of the best places to chill and chat in south Manchester. You can start at the beginning on the weekends here too, with a Full breakfast including drink (£8.95) or Smoked salmon and scrambled egg (£6.95). The evening menu features goodies such as Pan-fried fillet of hake (£14.50), which comes with a Basque peppers, salsa verde and crispy artichokes. There's also a good drinks range, wines, beers, juices and soft drinks. The bar may open later.

Food 4 Service 4 Décor 4

Vegetarian: several
Set menu: occasional such as a wine tasting menu (from £45)
Disabled access: full

After Eight £B

2 Edenfield Road, Rochdale

01706 646 432

www.aftereight.uk.com

Thu-Sat 7pm-9.30pm; Sun 12.30pm-3pm

This Rochdale institution is run by Geoff and Anne Taylor, who haven't let their perpetual place in the *Good Food Guide* and a *Michelin Guide* entry go to their heads. Here you'll find high-quality cuisine with a regularly changing menu. At time of press, good examples included Trio of fish and tartare sauce (£6), a perfectly Roasted brill with a brioche and herb crust (£15.80), Fillet of beef (£16.90) served on roasted Mediterranean vegetables with parsnip duchess potatoes and an English mustard pancake, and the Scottish dessert of Creme crowdie (£4) - a combination of fresh raspberries, oatmeal, whisky, honey and cream that tastes as good as it sounds. The traditional British farmhouse cheese range is spectacular - we dare you to finish it. The building is of sturdy stone outside with an ebullient and colourful interior.

Food 4 Service 5 Décor 4

Children: kids welcome, smaller portions available
Set menu: Sun lunches from £14.95
Vegetarian: separate menu
Disabled access: partial

British - Modern British

Albert's Shed £B

Castle Street, City

0161 839 9818 2G

www.albertsshed.com

Mon 5.30pm-10pm; Tue-Fri noon-2.30pm, 5.30pm-10pm; Sat noon- 11pm; Sun noon-9.30pm

Attached to established pub and eaterie Dukes 92 (see pg 125), this is a swish and smart addition to former bookie Jim Ramsbottom's property portfolio. Given the classy design, the name is perhaps too cutesy, referring to the site's former use as Uncle Albert Ramsbottom's storeroom. The food provides an Anglo-Mediterranean mix of dishes, from the splendid Albert's breakfast (£4.50) with potato cake, black pudding and a poached egg with a helping of home-made brown sauce to salads, pizzas and à la carte material such as Chargrilled steak (8oz fillet or 12oz rib eye) with all the trimmings. A big plus is the glorious and tranquil Castlefield setting, which makes Albert's Shed perfect for fine dining or corporate lunches.

Food 4 Service 3.5 Décor 4

Children: welcome, separate menu
Vegetarian: 4 starters and 4/5 mains plus pizza options
Set menus: lunchtime specials include 1 course for £6.50 and 2 courses for £8.95
Disabled access: full

Amba Restaurant and Lounge £B

106-108 Ashley Road, Hale, Cheshire

0161 928 2343

www.amba.uk.com

11am-11pm

Amba is consistently good with reasonable prices. The décor makes for convivial surroundings in chocolate and mocha and the clientele are flash - a bit like Hale itself. But good news travels fast and booking is recommended on Fri/Sat nights. The menu is extensive and caters for many different palates, with specials such as Marinated organic Cumbrian lamb steak with sauté potatoes and nectarine relish (£9.50) or Dutch calves liver with smoked bacon, gilded apples potato puree and sage jus (£10.50). These dish descriptions show the ambition (or maybe the amba-bition) of the place, but they do hint at an occasional over-complicated approach - not a problem unique to this venue alone, of course.

Food 4 Service 4 Décor 4

Entertainment: occasional
Children: numerous dishes, including tapas and smaller portions to order
Vegetarian: several dishes
Set menus: 6pm-7pm, 2 courses £11.95, 3 courses £14.95
Disabled access: partial

Beluga Restaurant £B

2 Mount Street, City

0161 833 3339 5E

www.belugaonline.co.uk

Mon-Thu 11am-10pm; Fri-Sat 11am-11pm; Bar Thu-Sat open until 2am

Housed in the handsome former Inland Revenue building of Manchester (note the lovely external sculptures of the lion and the unicorn), this is an easy-going and popular downtown rendezvous. The ground floor houses a bar with a streetside terrace, while downstairs is the restaurant. Good wholesome food is found in both places, for instance the Chorizo chicken and roast chilli squash (£11.95) and the Roasted red pepper en croute (£6.95), which is filled with cheese, peppers and spinach and served on a warm salad of pak choi and cherry tomato, new potatoes and a sun dried tomato and basil dressing. The Eton mess (£5.95) of meringue, strawberries and whipped cream is a lush way to conclude.

Food 3.5 Service 4 Décor 3.5

Entertainment: evening DJs at the weekends
Children: welcome but no menu
Set menu: from £16.95

wagamama

British - Modern British

The Market Restaurant £A/B

104 High Street, City

0161 834 3743 9B

www.market-restaurant.com

Wed-Sat noon-2.30pm, 7pm-9.30pm

The *City Life* Manchester Food and Drink Festival Restaurant of the Year 2005 provides one of the most enjoyable dining experiences in the city. To make things happen, you have to work at them, and after 25 years the Market still provides a template of how an independent, proprietor-driven business should operate. It has also been a torch bearer for the Northern Quarter. When this place opened, the potential of the area had been recognised, but few had dared to commit cash. The Market led the way and now sits proud on the most interesting food and drink street in North West England. The building the business occupies is a handsome late-Georgian brick delight. The interior is eclectic, colourful and above all, immediately comfortable. The evening appearance has been improved by the removal of the curtains from the windows, allowing a glimpse into that cosy interior. Service is led by Peter and Ann O'Grady and is knowledgeable and amiable in equal measure. The food from Paul Mertz and Mary-Rose Edgecombe is constantly interesting and occasionally touches on perfection. The eclectic dishes include Pork terrine with French bread and gherkins (£5.95), Fillet of salmon with herb crust on braised aubergine and red pepper sauce (£14.95) and Lemon curd jelly with almond shortbread served with a jug of cream (£4.95). The lunch menu is very competitive and again provides top-quality food. The Market uses local produce where possible and guarantees that everything from the biscuits to the ice cream is freshly made. There's a good wine list, but perhaps more intriguingly an exceptional selection of continental beers and even a martini list. Meanwhile, the specialist clubs for starters and puddings are real occasions - check the website. As an added bonus, the Market produces its own quarterly newsletter. Put simply, if you like food and you live in Manchester, you'll eventually find the Market.

Food 4.5 Service 4.5 Décor 4

Entertainment: occasional, such as Sweet Meets, the celebrated pudding club

Children: smaller portions available

Vegetarian: several (nominated in the Best Provision for Vegetarians category at the Food and Drink Festival 2005)

Disabled access: partial

GLAMOROUS
CHINESE RESTAURANT
HONG KONG STYLE

WING YIP BUSINESS CENTRE, 1st & 2nd FLOOR, OLDHAM ROAD, ANCOATS, MANCHESTER M4 5HU

TEL: 0161 839 3312 Fax: 0161 833 2798

OPENING HOURS
**SUN 11AM TO 11PM • MON-THURS 11.30AM TO 11.30PM
FRI & SAT 11.30AM TO 12 MIDNIGHT**

SPECIAL LUNCH TIME MENU FROM £5.95(per person)
MON - FRI (EXCEPT BANK HOLIDAY MONDAY)
ALSO, DIM SUM TROLLEY AVAILABLE SUN, MON & TUE

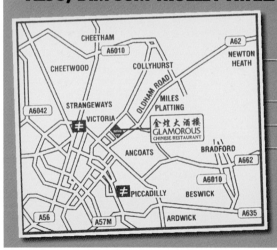

300 FREE PARKING SPACES WITH 24HR SECURITY

PRIVATE FUNCTION ROOM SEATS 200

AIR CONDITIONED

KARAOKE AVAILABLE

2 FLOORS -
200 UPSTAIRS, 400 DOWNSTAIRS

Charles Hallé Restaurant £B

Bridgewater Hall, Lower Mosley Street, City

0161 907 9000 5F

From 5.30pm on concert nights - one sitting only

A visit here needs to be combined with a concert in this state-of-the-art hall. This is a restaurant that you can't wander into from the street - it is more of a specialist night out. But the food from Marco Tedde can be exceptional, which is why the place gets included in this book. Dinner comes via two courses plus coffee at £17.50, or three courses plus coffee at £22.50. A recent *City Life* visit included in the set menu a Fillet of sea bass with crayfish and rice, which was a winner. The fish was light but distinctive, and the crayfish bolstered the flavours whilst the cooked-to-perfection pilau rice, lifted by coriander, had a scent that pushed you to nirvana. It's for these qualities that you might elect to share the spick and span modern space of the Bridgewater Hall with retired colonels, lecturers, accountants and their respective partners on a big night out.

Food 4 Service 3 Décor 3

Vegetarian: dishes with every set menu

Set menu: see above

Disabled access: full

Isinglass £B

46 Flixton Road, Urmston

0161 749 8400

Tue-Sun 6pm-10.30pm; Fri-Sun noon-5.30pm

Every suburb needs a place like Isinglass: an innovative and well-run restaurant that combines good service with great value and a tasteful appearance. It's got principles too - throughout the menu, places such as Holly Tree Farm in Knutsford are name-checked. And the hearty local origins of the food explains the hearty nature of the dishes. On a changing menu on one *City Life* visit, the starter of Victorian potted beef (£4.65) with summer pickled veg and organic bread was an example of this, a solid dish of strapping flavour and big textures. The mains continued the theme. The Belly pork (£9.95) came in juniper and bay with a fat spud, sage stuffing fritters and so on. It was a succulent, lip-smackingly good dish. For dessert, the Knickerbocker glory (£3.95) worked completely. The drinks range is excellent too. The wine list criss-crosses the globe with variety and interest, whilst care has also been taken to provide good bottled beer such as St Peter's Organic Ale - why don't more people do this? If Isinglass has a problem, it's that the gung-ho approach can lead to a lack of finesse. If the restaurant can work on some very hard edges in its dishes whilst remaining faithful to its principles, it will soar higher.

Food 4 Service 4 Décor 4

Children: very welcome, separate menus/highchairs/toys

Vegetarian: several options including vegan

Disabled access: full

British - Modern British

Café Jem&I £B

1c School Lane, Didsbury

0161 445 3996

Mon 5.30pm-10pm; Tue-Fri 11.30am-2.30pm, 5.30pm-10pm; Sat 9.30am-3pm, 6pm-10pm; Sun noon-3pm, 5.30pm-10pm

Jem O'Sullivan, with his eponymous restaurant, has over the last couple of years ensured that Didsbury village has at least one independent to compete with precocious West Didsbury. Despite the unexceptional exterior, inside this place is comfortable if simple. The main feature is a shiny metal bar, with the wine behind, and next to that is a tiny kitchen. A signature dish is the Aged 10oz Scotch Sirloin steak served with sautéed mushrooms, fat chips and a choice of two sauces (£13.95). If you want an idea of what a decent little independent restaurant should be doing, Café Jem&I is a good place to start.

Food 4 Service 4 Décor 3

Children: dishes on request, served half price
Vegetarian: 3 starters, 2 mains.
Set menus: 3 course Sunday lunch £14.95.
Disabled access: partial

Obsidian Bar and Restaurant £A/B

18-24 Princess Street, City

0161 238 4348 6E

www.obsidianmanchester.co.uk

Daily noon-2.30pm; Mon-Sat 6pm-10.30pm; Sun 6pm-9.30pm. Light snacks and tapas available at the bar

The *City Life* Newcomer of the Year 2004, and despite the strange geological name - obsidian is a black volcanic rock - it's got the looks, the food, the drink and the service. The first feature to grab the attention is the bar counter filled with a thousand illuminated rectangles, like a frozen Pearl and Dean ad for the 21st century. Then the eye settles on the calm restaurant with its leather booths. Chef Duncan Poyser prepares robust food with exquisite nuances of flavour in generous portions. Occasionally he almost seems to flirt with coarseness. Take the home-made bread, which is a triumph of texture and fibre - you could live for a week just by eating one loaf. If you had to choose a speciality/signature dish, it is perhaps the Monk fish tandoori with spiced chick peas, grilled lime and coriander butter (£18.95). The wine list gives a good selection of often more unusual reds and wines. The bar is run as a separate strand of Obsidian. The Obsidian cocktail (£6.50) takes the colour of the rock as its base and delivers a rich blackberry kick of black pepper, vodka and Tabasco. There are excellent and lighter lunchtime options available, including tapas, soups, salads and sandwiches.

Food 4.5 Service 4 Décor 4

Entertainment: occasional
Children: welcome
Vegetarian: several options from tapas to mains plus a complete vegan/vegetarian menu
Set menus: 2 courses £12, 3 courses £16
Disabled access: full

British - Modern British

Choice £B

Castle Quay, Castlefield, City

0161 833 3400 2G

www.choicemcr.co.uk

Mon-Sun 11am-11pm

This is a proper award winner being 2003 *City Life* Restaurant of the Year and the 2002 Manchester Food and Drink Festival winner of the Best Wine List. It has a splendid position on the Castlefield canal basin and a simple, elegant interior that is warmed by the exposed brick and the comfortable sisal carpet. The space is divided in two - bar and restaurant - with a piano in the bar area for weekend smoothie music. Good food options on the seasonal menu which illustrate the variety available include Haddock fillet (£15.95), garlic and citrus marinated haddock, warm salad of new potatoes, roast tomatoes , green beans and rough cut chilli or Cottage Pie (£14.95), beef fillet, root veg, thyme gravy, creamed potato and Lancashire cheese. The focus where possible is on North West produce and Choice works closely with regional producers .

Food 4 Service 4 Décor 4

Entertainment: piano music on Sat
Children: smaller portions
Vegetarian: 2 starters, 2 mains
Set menus: Mon-Fri before 4pm and Sun lunch before 6pm, 2 courses £12.95, 3 courses £15.95
Disabled access: full

Grinch 6D

Chapel Walks, City

0161 907 3210

www.grinch.co.uk

Mon-Sat noon-11pm; Sun noon-10.30pm

In the fickle world of restaurant and bars Neil Lawrence and Ged Lynch are canny operators who know their market extremely well - they've even expanded their horizons with the Felicini mini-chain (see Italian below). Grinch, though, is a city centre one off with a Cheers-like feel and the campest staff outside the village. The food is just what you'd expect too, a clever mixture of healthy Med-style dishes and a nod to trad British tastes plus over 21 cocktails. The menu changes frequently with a typical dish being the Fried chicken with fries and a barbeque dip (£8.95). Recently Grinch reintroduced their beans and toast special in a return to some retro favourites. Good cocktails.

Food 3.5 Service 4 Décor 3.5

Entertainment: Sat, live jazz and blues
Children: welcome
Vegetarian: several choices

Harts £B

7 Church Street, Leigh

01942 680 650

Weds to Sun 7pm till late (last food orders 9pm)

In this hidden gem in the heart of a culinary wasteland chef/proprietor Paul Hart has established a considerable reputation over the past 12 years. With only 30 covers it is a perfect replica of a Parisian bistro without any faux Gallic additions. The signature dish here is the Noisettes of Lamb, a boned loin sliced into noisettes and cooked in a sauce of home- grown blackberries (£10.50). The Parma Chicken stuffed with mozarella cheese and served in a rich mushroom and brandy sauce is also highly recommended (£10. 50). There is a chalked up specials board and a short seven item vegetarian menu. There is disabled access and group booking set- menus can be arranged with Paul starting at £20 per head. You can sip Ch Margaux 1990 from your own cellar with your meal for this is a "Bring Your Own" restaurant (corkage £1. 50 per bottle).

Food 4.5 Service 3 Décor 3

Children: welcome
Vegetarian: on request

British - Modern British

The Lime Tree £B

8 Lapwing Lane, West
Didsbury

0161 445 1217

www.thelimetreerestaurant.
co.uk

**Mon & Sat 5.45pm-10.15;
Tue-Fri noon-2.30pm, 5.45pm-
10.15pm; Sun noon- 2.30pm,
5.45pm-10pm**

One of the best restaurants in the
North West. The food is top notch,
the atmosphere easy going. The
Lime Tree is the anchor tenant in
terms of quality and aspiration for the
garden of delights that has become
the West Didsbury food and drink
scene. Signature dishes include
Grilled asparagus spears with
roasted red pepper, goats cheese
and tomato vinaigrette (£5.75),
Crispy roast duckling with orange
sauce and seasonal vegetables
(£12.95) and a ridiculously rich
sticky toffee pudding (£4.75). The
dining room is a convivial space
with attached conservatory and new
outdoor dining area.

Food 4.5 Service 3 Décor 4

Children: smaller portions of items
on menu. Children's menu on Sun -
£10.95 for 3 courses and coffee

Vegetarian: at least one option

Set menu: noon-2.30pm, 5.45pm-
6.30pm, 3 courses £14.95; Sun
lunch £16.95

Disabled access: partial

Sam's Chop House £B

Back Pool Fold, Chapel Walks,
off Cross Street, City

0161 834 3210 6D

www.samschophouse.co.uk

Mon-Sat 11am-11pm

Whether it's from experience,
Hollywood movies, the novels of
Charles Dickens or a thousand
other sources, everyone in the world
has a picture of the ideal English
inn. The name of that inn can now
be revealed: Sam's Chophouse.
The delightful basement location,
rich in timber and tile, is split into
pub and restaurant - and you'll be
comfortable in either. The food is
classic British cuisine that manages
to somehow be contemporary at the
same time. Sam's is the brother of
Mr Thomas's on Cross Street (see
pubs section) and both are under
the excellent tutelage of Steve
Pilling, Roger Ward and chef Phillip
Nellis. Menu choices include rib of
beef, leg of lamb or pork carved

at the table, or Homemade corned
beef hash (£11.95). Other signatures
are Fish pie with cheese and chive
sauce (£12.94) and the Muffin hot
pot with pickled red cabbage and
beetroot (£12.95). The puds are
lovely and the local cheeses superb.
The wine list is as good as any in the
region (complete with wine club too)
and there is even an in-house ale.
Visitors from all quarters of the world
adore Sam's too for the blast of
gorgeous British cooking it provides.
Indeed, in a city where you can dine
for 30 days without covering the
same style of national cuisine, it's in
the traditional areas of indigenous
cooking that we frequently lose
out. It must be these qualities that
have appealed to a whole roster of
famous guests, from artist LS Lowry
to stars of stage, screen and sports
field.

Food 4.5 Service 4 Décor 5

Entertainment: occasional

Children: some dishes at a reduced
price/smaller portion.

Vegetarian: at least 2 starters and
2 mains

British - Modern British

Nutters £B/A

Edenfield Road (A680),
Norden, Rochdale

01706 650167

Tue-Sat noon-2pm, afternoon tea
3pm-5pm, 6.30pm-9.30pm; Sun
noon-4pm, 6.30pm-9pm

Nutters is now located in new and
vast premises, a former Victorian
mansion with 6.5 acres of land.
Chef/proprietor Andrew Nutter's
ambitions are in evidence in the
series of branded condiments and
even teddy bears for sale close to
the entrance. The food is still more
than worth the journey to these
distant frontiers of the conurbation.
Try starters of Chicken liver parfait
with pistachio chunks and port
reduction (£5.50) or mains such as
the sensational Flash seared beef
fillet with potato bonbon, served
with caramelised onions and a light
tarragon and green peppercorn
(£16.95). The signature of Crispy
Bury black pudding wantons with
confetti of vegetables (£6.50)
remains on the menu. The gourmet
menu is a real experience.

Food 4 Service 4 Décor 4

Entertainment: occasional
Children: smaller portions available
Set menu: Gourmet Menu, 6
courses £32 pp; Sun special noon-
4pm 3 courses £19.95
Vegetarian: several options
Disabled access: full

Old Wellington Restaurant and Inn £B/C

New Cathedral Gate, City

0161 830 1440 6B

**Mon-Sat 11am-11pm
(restaurant 11.30am-9pm);
Sun noon-10.30pm (restaurant
noon-5pm)**

Beloved of a thousand postcards,
this classic Manchester building
dating from 1530s was once all pub
but is now more restaurant. There
is still a bar downstairs, but both
the charming upper floors are food
only. The best of the bunch is the
top floor, with its low beams padded
to stop you cracking your skull.
The restaurant was painstakingly
dismantled and rebuilt here after the
IRA bomb of 1996. A signature dish
for the Old Wellington might be the
Fillet of beef Wellington with roasted
vegetables and a redcurrant port
sauce (£14.95). By the way, you sit
with real history here, the building
having witnessed the march of
Bonnie Prince Charlie into the town
in 1745 and much else besides.

Food 3.5 Service 4 Décor 5

Children: light bites or smaller
portions
Vegetarian: 3 mains, 4 salads
Set menu: 3 courses £12.95
Disabled access: partial

The Restaurant Bar and Grill £B

14 John Dalton Street, City

0161 839 1999 5D

**Mon-Fri noon-3pm, 6pm-11pm;
Sat noon-11pm; Sun noon-
10.30pm**

Specialising in modern comfort
food, the Restaurant Bar and Grill is
never short of diners, particularly in
the arching glass canopied section
out front. Classy pasta dishes and
upmarket burgers and salads are
well loved alongside stand-out
treats like their Swordfish steak on a
bed of salted avocado (£13.95), cut
through with a citrussy mango relish
and Lamb tikka with lentil, mint and
tomato salad (£14.50), a civilised
take on kebab shop cuisine. Starters
are equally good, in particular the
seasonal likes of Summer pea and
scallop soup (£5.50), and they
make their ice creams in house.
This businessman's favourite is a
bit like a grown-up version of TGI
Fridays, only with a well-chosen
wine list and attentive service.

Food 4 Service 3 Décor 3

Children: smaller portions of menu
dishes
Vegetarian: starter and main
Disabled access: full

British - Modern British

Bit of a mouthful

The following notice appeared in a Manchester newspaper on June 11, 1754: 'Mr Powell, the Fire-Eater, who lately exhibited his Performances, had the Misfortune to burn his Mouth in a terrible Manner; not in perfoming any of his various and amzing curiosities, but in eating of a hot Apple-Pye to his supper.' Let's hope it was a good pie.

Eighteenth century Manchester adored eating. One group showed their appreciation of this fundamental human joy by starting a society with exclusive membership: the Club for Fat Men. Membership was not gained by the amount somebody weighed but by the following sneaky test. Those who wished to join had to be too large to fit, without turning sideways, through a specially constructed extra-wide door. Another favoured pastime was to gamble on the amount you could put away - very *Cool Hand Luke*. A hundred years or so ago, a gentleman, north of the city, for a bet 'ate three pounds of porridge, one quart of water, one pint of milk, one quart of a small drink, two oat cakes, nine pounds of cowhead without the bone, four quarts of water, one quart of ale, three oat and seven penny pies'. He won the bet.

As recently as 1973, Mancunian James Lindop ate 13 raw eggs in 3.8 seconds, whilst a year later, in Manchester's Post Office Social Club, Nigel Moore took just 30 seconds to eat 1,823 cold beans one by one, using a cocktail stick. Well done Nigel. You fool.

Rhubarb £B

167 Burton Road, West Didsbury

0161 448 8887

www.rhubarbrestaurant.co.uk

Tue-Sat 5pm-10pm; Sun 1pm-8.30pm (last food orders)

Chef Mark Ramsden set up Rhubarb with his wife Lisa in 2003 (winning the *City Life* Newcomer of the Year Award) and the pair continue to present top-quality seasonal dishes that are sure to impress anyone, from humble visiting relative to eminent food critic. For a true sense of the establishment's prowess, try the Pan-fried fillet of sea bass (£13.95), served with a new potato and crème fraiche salad, and a salsa of olives, roast peppers and red onions - an astonishing dish that is as original and intense as Rhubarb's deep red back wall. The Porcini mushroom risotto, available as a starter and a main (£5.50/£11.95), also comes highly recommended. And make sure you save room for dessert, where Rhubarb makes use of its namesake in a famous crème brûlée (£4.95).

Food 4.5 Service 4 Décor 4

Children: smaller portions
Vegetarian: 2 mains, 2/3 starters
Set menus: early evening special Tue-Sat 5pm-6.30pm & Sun 1pm-6.30pm, 2 courses £12.95, 3 courses £15.95

Saints Brasserie

St Mary's Gate, Uppermill Village, Saddleworth

01457 875 025

Tue-Sun from 6.30pm

A *City Life* favourite in the hills, Saints Brasserie is a real, 24-cover find in a converted café. Dishes greatly enjoyed have included a nicely balanced Mezze of bruschetta, olives, houmous, pitta and allioli (£5.95 to share), a Wild mushroom risotto cake with sauce tomaté and pesto (£4.50), Suckling pig with apple and truffle salad accompanied by raspberry syrup (£6.50), a splendidly cooked slice of Seabass with a novel chorizo, spinach, chickpeas and balsamic reduction (£12. 95), a Rump of lamb served with a simple bed of lightly herbed couscous and jus of olive (£12.95) and Apple tarte tatin with an intriguing Wensleydale and rosemary ice cream (£4.50). This is a small, comfortably intimate venture that is ready to be discovered by the rest of Greater Manchester, and the location in Uppermill under the epic Pennine moors is a bonus.

Food 4.5 Service 4.5 Décor 4

Children: welcome, half price options
Vegetarian: several options

British - Modern British

Simply Heathcote's £B

Jacksons Row, off Deansgate, City

0161 835 3536 4E

www.heathcotes.co.uk

Mon-Sun noon-2.30pm; Mon-Fri 5.30pm-10pm; Sat 5.30-11pm; Sun noon-9pm

Heathcote's is a good, professionally run, up-market mini-chain. Visually it is a smart city centre operation too, with a sharp, modern interior. Starters (the menu changes seasonally) might include Heathcote's black pudding and muffin with dry cured bacon, poached egg and hollandaise (£6), while mains might have a range of pasta, risotto and veggie dishes (around £10) as well as fish and poultry specialities. For a blowout, try the Curwen Hill chargrilled rump steak served with grilled Portobello mushrooms and balsamic roasted tomatoes (£14.50). For dessert, first-timers should have nothing other than the famous Heathcote's bread and butter pudding with apricot compote and clotted cream (£5).

Food 4 Service 4 Décor 4

Children: menu
Vegetarian: 5 starters, 4 mains
Service charge: 10%
Set menu: £11.95 or £15 on certain days
Disabled access: full

Stables Bistro

276 Stockport Road, Hyde

0161 366 0300

www.stablesbistro.co.uk

Although you may be disappointed to learn there's little in the way of actual ponies in this most horse-obsessed of restaurants, that should prove the only let-down. Situated in the picturesque village of Gee Cross, and bearing more than a slight resemblance to someone's front room, Stables and its sister venue Flamin' Nosh have built up a solid following. With equine images scattered on every available surface, it's no surprise that starters, mains and puddings (all three for £18.95) are labelled under the headers 'Grooming', 'Shoeing' and 'Sugar cubes'. Carrots and Polo mints notwithstanding, highlights include a Curried chicken and mango salad, Smoked salmon with balsamic dressing on croutons, followed by a generous Fillet of beef with red-hot chilli salsa and an equally meaty Sea bass and scallops. But, given the potent wine list, best leave Mr Ed outside, eh?

Food 4 Service 4 Décor 4

Entertainment: wine tasting, guest chefs
Children: welcome
Vegetarian: 2 starters, 1 main
Set menus: 3 courses for £18.95
Disabled access: full

That Café £B

1031 Stockport Road, Levenshulme

0161 432 4672

www.thatcafe.co.uk

Tue-Sat 6pm-10pm; Sun noon-2.30pm

Wonderfully independent little restaurant offering a competent, regularly changing menu to a loyal crowd. That Café is a scrubbed up conversion of a couple of red-bricked terraced houses on Levenshulme's main drag. Inside, all is calm: floral wallpaper, lived in sofas and simply set tables. Food is adventurous enough to lift the experience high above the commonplace, teaming artichoke hearts with blue cheese, lamb with Welsh rarebit and beetroot. Prices hover around £6.50 for starters, £15 for mains, yet still offer good value when the food is this lovingly prepared. Desserts, too, are memorable, offering such delights as Pear and almond tart served with a plum and lime sauce (£4.50).

Food 4.5 Service 4 Décor

Entertainment: jazz night, first Wed of month at 7.30pm
Children: dishes on request
Vegetarian: 8 starters, 8 main courses
Set menu: 6pm-7pm Tue-Fri, 2 courses £12.95
Disabled access: partial

British - Modern British

Caribbean

White Hart Inn

Stockport Road, Lydgate, Oldham

01457 872 566

www.thewhitehart.co.uk

Pub: Mon-Sat noon-11pm; Sun noon-10.30pm. Food Mon-Sat noon-2.30pm, 6pm-9.30pm; Sun 1pm-7.30pm

The multi awarding winning White Hart has graduated from a pub to a brasserie, restaurant and hotel in a fine setting overlooking Saddleworth. It's perhaps best known for local delicacies from the in-house Saddleworth Sausage Company, which can also be bought to take away, including traditional Cumberland, Manchester (spicy pork) and Wild boar (apple and sage). The three-course Sunday lunch (£19) is worth the excursion - book into the fine hotel to avoid the drive back and partake of the superb à la carte menu. Get a full flavour of the White Hart during one of its busy events, such as the Valentine's Dinner or 'Cheese Detective' tastings.

Food 4 Service 3.5 Décor 4

Entertainment: many tastings and special events - see website
Children: dishes available
Vegetarian: one set dish, other alternatives available on request
Set menu: 4 course £39.50, 3 course £34.50
Disabled access: full on ground floor

Caribbean round-up

Aside from Vernon's in Rusholme (see right), there's a range of Caribbean cuisine across the city, mainly available through take-aways and mobile units. *City Life* favourites include Sam Sam's (Greenhey's Lane, Hulme - behind McDougall Sports Hall, 226 7673), Jerk'n'Spiced (157A Princess Road, Moss Side, 226 6656), The Chicken Run (6a Yarburgh Street, Moss Side, 226 6714), Buzz Rocks, (Hulme Market, off Hulme High Street), Cool Runnings (take-away van, junction of Chorlton Road and Cornbrook Street, Hulme), Dougy's (Brook's Bar, Moss Lane West, Hulme, 226 9500) and M&M's Caribbean Spice (127 Stamford Street, Old Trafford, 226 6067). This last is a proper sit-down café with a take-away, delivery and catering service. There's an excellent choice including Curried mutton, Fried fish, and Jerk Chicken. Most of these come with Rice'n'peas - the staple filler of Caribbean cuisine. The speciality soups are definitely moreish

Vernon's Caribbean Restaurant

2 Wilmslow Road, Rusholme

0870 220 0560

www.vernosjackparadise.co.uk

Tue-Fri noon-11pm; Sat 3pm-11pm; Sun 4pm-10pm (times may vary during winter months)

V's is run by Pete Vernon, son of Allan - who's famous in culinary circles for taking jerk seasoning to New York over 20 years ago and for his bottled condiments. It is a contemporary, clean, non-smoking, space. Starters included Fried plantain (large, softly sweet banana, £2), Fish and Vegetable patties (various ingredients having been 'patted down' to gently fry, both £1.50) and Festivals (£1.50). These are Vernon's own speciality dumplings mixed to perfection to avoid any cloying heaviness. Main courses include Oxtail (£10.50), Curried goat (£10.50), Escovitch fish (£10.50) and Jerk chicken (£9), with side orders of Rice and peas and Candied yams (£2.50 each). The jerk is Vernon's own seasoning, and is suitably sensational.

Food 3.5 Service 3 Décor 3

Entertainment: jazz every Wed 7.30pm-10.30pm
Children: very welcome, separate menu plus a choice of smaller portions from the adult menu
Vegetarian: 9 starters, 20 mains
Disabled access: full

Chinatown

Based around the Chinese Arch, the ornate red and gold structure that was erected as a symbol of the friendship between the Chinese people and Manchester in 1987, Chinatown is now the centre for the North's Chinese community.

Restaurants moved in during the '70s when the warehouses fell into disuse, and now old people's homes, acupuncture clinics and supermarkets are all bundled in together beside the restaurants and take-aways to make one of the city's most interesting quarters.

Indulging in a mooch around the area can be hungry work, and aside from the separate entries on Chinese dining in this section, other restaurants you might opt to visit whilst in the area include the new Hong Kong (0161 236 7003), the Peking Court (0161 236 5236), the Wong Chu (0161 236 2346) and the oldest in the area, the Woo Sang (0161 236 3697).

Watch out for the key festivals on the Chinese calendar - each of these has its own food. Chinese New Year, which falls on 29 January in 2006, inspires a party atmosphere in the city and includes the famous procession with the block-long dragon. Associated foods are fish, cooked whole to represent togetherness, and chicken, prepared with the head, tail and feet to symbolise completeness. Another date to look out for is the Mid-Autumn Festival, 18 September 2005, which is celebrated with fire-crackers and the like. Moon-cakes, the speciality food, are very sweet and come in a lucky red box.

When your yin and yang are off-kilter, traditional Chinese medicinal treatments are readily available from centres such as Shanghai on Portland Street. Expect to pay around £25 for acupuncture and from £10 for a diagnosis and traditional herbal remedy. Note that the Chinese Arts Centre is not in Chinatown, rather in the Market Buildings on Thomas Street, but is worth a visit nonetheless.

Three tips while your exploring the area: a legendary Honey bun from Ho's Bakery (Faulkner Street) should be sampled (try to catch them while they're still warm). Delve into one of the supermarkets, brim-full of Chinese fare, such as the wonderful Hang Won Hong on George Street. And slip inside T.La Art and Craft Shop where a den of paper parasols, music boxes and other inexpensive goodies will tempt you into leaving with something you never thought you needed.

Not everything is rosy about Chinatown though - the feng shui must be out of wack. At present, new smart Chinese restaurants seem to want to open outside the streets that make up Chinatown. Perhaps this means that the area is in decline or perhaps simply that restaurants want to be judged on their own merits rather than being bracketed with the mass of good but not exceptional Chinese establishments around Nicholas Street and Faulkner Street. Or perhaps there just isn't room within for the bigger floorplates people require within the district. A similar process is taking place in the Asian dining area of Rusholme. Time will tell how the situation works out.

Chinese glossary

Bamboo shoots: The young, edible shoots of certain bamboo.

Bao ji (manapua): Stuffed baked or steamed buns.

Beancurd (tofu): Discovered during the Han dynasty (206 BC - AD 220). A white, squishy substance from ground yellow soybeans; an alternative to meat.

Black beans: Small, black soy beans preserved by being cooked and fermented with salt and spices, used in dishes from Southern China.

Bok choy: Chinese white cabbage.

Char sui: Barbecued pork.

Chop sui: Odds and ends - served with rice or soy sauce.

Chow fun: Wide, stir-fried noodles.

Chow mein: Stir-fried, thin, wheat-noodle dishes.

Chung choy: Preserved turnip.

Coriander (hong choi): Known as Chinese parsley, coriander has a pungent flavour and is one of the few herbs used in Chinese cooking.

Crack seed: Dried fruit with seasoning.

Dim sum: Small snacks, dumplings that are baked, fried or steamed.

Fortune cookies: Tiny crisp cookies containing paper messages detailing 'your fortune'. Their origins are in the Chinese 49-ers who worked on the building of the great American railways.

Fu young: Scrambled dishes.

Hoi sin sauce: Thick, sweet bean paste, often with Peking duck.

Jook (congee): Rice soup.

Lychee: A round, white fruit often eaten for dessert.

Mooncake: Originating from the 13th and 14th century when China was occupied by the Mongols. These cakes, made of lotus nut paste with an egg in the middle, are eaten at special occasions.

Noodles: They play an important part in Chinese tradition as they symbolise longevity. If you cut them, it is said to shorten your life. They are mainly made from wheat or rice flour and water (in Southern China, egg is added). The skill of noodle making takes five years to perfect.

Oyster sauce: A traditional thick, brown sauce with extract of oysters.

Rice wine: Wine made from rice, yeast and spring water.

Seaweed: Dried bok choy, sliced very thinly and deep-fried. Served as an accompaniment.

Sesame prawn toasts: Prawns mashed and layered on toast, coated in sesame seeds and deep fried.

Soy sauce: Made from soybeans, flour and water in two varieties, either dark or light. A thousand years ago, soy sauce was one of the seven essentials of Chinese daily life.

Star anise: The hard, star-shaped seed pod of as tree that grows in Western China.

Sweet and sour sauce: A tangy red sauce popular with the Western palate, made with rice wine, vinegar, sugar, cornflour, tomato and soy sauce. Typically eaten with prawns or deep-fried battered pork or chicken.

Sweetcorn soup: Hot, heavy soup from the Szechuan region, often eaten as a starter.

Szechuan: A region of China, boasting a fine cusine.

Tofu: See beancurd.

Tree ears: A dry fungus, soaked before cooking.

Tsing dao: Great Chinese beer.

Water chestnuts: A sweet, white, crunchy water vegetable. Sliced into thin circles and cooked.

Wontons: Dumplings wrapped in fine wonton dough. Delicious deep fried or added to soups.

Glamorous Restaurant £B

Wing Yip, Thompson Street,
off Oldham Road, Ancoats

0161 839 3312

Mon-Thu 11am-11.30pm; Fri-Sun 11.30am-midnight

It's the extraordinary décor that
makes it worthy of inclusion
here. Because the Glamourous
Restaurant lives up to its name with
the craziest collection of plastic tack
ever assembled in a city eaterie.
It has to be seem to be believed,
although a dead give-away of what
lies within comes via three plastic
flashing coconut trees on the roof
above the car park. The silliness
continues inside, with the biggest
view from the windows being of
the adjacent multi-storey car park.
The place always seems busy
and is popular with the Chinese
community. The food is predictable,
but Glamorous is worth a visit for
the décor - sort of Oldham Road
Las Vegas - and there's always the
marvellous Chinese supermarket
below.

Food 3 Service 3 Décor 5 or 0

Children: dishes on request
Vegetarian: variety of vegetarian
options plus a vegetarian banquet
Set menu: banquet £15.50
Disabled access: full

Red Chilli £B

70-72 Portland Street, City

0161 236 2888

www.redchillirestaurant.co.uk

**Mon-Thu noon-11pm; Fri-Sat
noon-midnight; Sun noon-11pm**

This snazzy, sub-street-level Chinese
restaurant combines some of the
area's finest food with originality
and flair. The bright, cheery
decorations include bird and flower
glass panel lights suspended from
above, while square mirrors line
the walls - indicating a thankfully
high ambition to offer something
different to the norm. And in a city
where Cantonese cuisine means
Far East cuisine, Red Chilli provides
the welcome alternative of authentic
Beijing and Szechuan dishes. Be
prepared to go exotic, or at least
exotic from a Western point of view,
with a selection of cold starters,
such as Red hot chilli pork stomach
shreds (£4) and Poached tofu
with sesame oil and spring onion

(£4). The restaurant specialises in
seafood - try the Crispy seabass
with sweet vinegar (£12) or the
entertainingly titled Crispy yellow
croaker with tomato sauce (£12) for
a truly individual treat. Vegetables
are also exceptional, particularly
the Beijing pak-choi (£6.50). And if
you're feeling more chilly than chilli,
look no further than the Lamb and
molly clay pot (£7.50), which is a
thin yet hearty stew. Or for a more
exotic treat, try the Husband and
wife lung slices (£4) - we're teasing
here, so you'll just have to go along
yourself to find out what this is. A
recommended signature dish is the
Hot and spicy poached sea bass
(£12). Red Chili is simply wonderful
and an unexpected treat.

Food 4.5 Service 4 Décor 4

Children: welcome
Vegetarian: 9 starters, 11 mains,
1 banquet
Set menus: 3/4 course banquets
from £22-£26 per person

Chinese

Little Yang Sing £B

17 George Street, City

0161 228 7722 7E

www.littleyangsing.co.uk

Mon-Thu noon-midnight; Fri noon-12.30am; Sat noon-1am; Sun noon-11pm

Its nomination for *City Life* Restaurant of the Year 2004 shows how this handsome Chinatown destination restaurant has embedded itself within the city dining scene. The décor is neither faddy feng shui nor drenched in dragons. Instead, an individual maroon padded banquette takes up the right hand side of the wall and is inset with a miniature terracotta army. Dim sums include the glorious Ow yuk dumpling (£2.50), steamed beef balls with ginger and spring onion, and other choice dishes include the Beancurd waffle with spicy vegetable (£4) and the Salt and pepper squid (£9). The quality of service is high.

Food 4 Service 4 Décor 4

Entertainment: none
Children: welcome, lunchtime menu
Vegetarian: 40 dishes
Service charge: 10%
Set menu: at all times, 3 courses £16pp; noon-6pm, 2 courses £8.50, 3 courses £10.50 (Sat noon-5); banquets from £21.50pp
Disabled access: partial

Moso Moso £B

403-419 Oxford Road, University

0161 273 3373

www.mosomoso.co.uk

Sun-Thu 10am-midnight; Fri–Sat 10am-2am

Moso Moso covers both Chinese and Thai cuisine in a menu as extensive as its contemporary premises. The impressive wine list shows proprietor Raymond Wong's passion for the grape. Dim sum starters such as Beef dumplings with ginger and spring onions (£2.20) and Sweet lotus cream buns (£2.20) are all very good. An alternative is to try the superb Baked mussels with garlic butter and Thai herbs (£6). For mains, you can't go wrong with Monkfish in a lemon and honey sauce (£9.50), the Chicken yellow curry (£7) or the Char siu roast pork (£6). Moso Moso is lively and likeable.

Food 4 Service 3.5 Décor 4

Entertainment: Sun and Mon salsa classes 6pm
Vegetarian: 3-page vegetarian menu plus a vegetarian banquet
Service charge: 10%
Set menus: 2 person banquet £16.50, 4 person banquet £29.50
Children: very welcome, Sat is family day - 25% off all day for families
Disabled access: full

Wing's Restaurant £B

1 Lincoln Square, City

0161 834 9000 5D

www.wingsrestaurant.co.uk

Mon-Sat noon-midnight; Sun noon-10pm

Wing's might be new, but the management aren't fresh to the food game, having run a respected restaurant in Cheadle Hulme for many years. Chef Wing Shing Chu has even made it on to TV - although these days it seems that most chefs have. Located in the old Lincoln restaurant, the décor has been subtly updated with an Oriental twist. The wine choice is dazzling. Dishes *City Life* have enjoyed include the Seafood dim sum platter (£6.80) as a starter with a side order of Seaweed (£3.40), Steamed lo han (fresh and dried vegetables) dumplings (£2.60), the exceptional Shanghai hot chilli lamb (£8.90) and the Ma pop tofu (£7.90) with soft noodles and silver sprout soft noodles (£4.40).

Food 4 Service 4 Décor 4

Children: welcome
Vegetarian: many options and veggie set menu
Service charge: 10%
Set menus: banquet A £20.90, banquet B £26.90, seafood banquet £34.90 - see website
Disabled access: partial

Tai Pan £B

Brunswick House, 81-
97 Upper Brook Street,
University

0161 273 2798

www.taipan.co.uk

**Mon-Sat noon-11.30pm; Sun
11.30am- 9.30pm**

This was the first of the Chinese
concept supermarkets meets
restaurants on one of the arterial
routes out of the city. It's been a
success story from the beginning.
Tai Pan may look like Hyacinth
Bouquet's house in *Keeping Up
Appearances*, but the food is good
- possibly because there's a huge
Chinese supermarket downstairs
supplying fresh and interesting
foods throughout the year. Like an
Ikea for Chinese food, it's worth a
visit in its own right. Particularly of
interest is the restaurant's dizzying
array of Dim sum (prices range from
£2.80-£4.60) that are presented
on a separate menu (sweet,
steamed and fried). The two-course
business lunch (£5.95) takes place
Mon-Fri from noon-2pm and is
recommended.

Food 3.5 Service 3.5 Décor 2

Children: welcome

Vegetarian: large selection plus a
vegetarian banquet (£18.50)

Set menus: from £5.95, banquets
start at £20 per person

Disabled access: partial

Tai Wu £B

44 Oxford Street, City

0161 236 6557 6F

www.tai-wu.com

Daily noon-2.45am

Unappetisingly lurking under a
multi-storey car park, the Tai Wu
is pleasantly, tastefully and yet
vigorously dressed out in a mix of
beige-white, scarlets and rosewood.
Service is attentive for all and
welcoming for families. A nice touch
is the space between the tables,
which allows customers plenty of
elbow room. The food is good - very
good in the dim sums, with the Beef
dumpling with ginger and spicy
onion (£2.40) being superb. Whilst
mains such as the Fried sliced
lamb (£8) and the Roast belly pork
(£8.50) are also excellent. A special
treat is the Baked lobster with
ginger and spring onion (£15.50),
and also recommended is the
Peking aromatic crispy duck (£8 for
¼). There's a good wine list to be
enjoyed while you take in the view
of the passing throngs and buses
on one of Manchester's busiest
streets.

Food 3.5 Service 4 Décor 3.5

Children: on request, flexible

Vegetarian: various dishes plus a
vegetarian banquet £17.50

Set menus: from £17.50-£26.50

Disabled access: full

Yang Sing £B/A

34 Princess Street, City

0161 236 2200 7E

www.yang-sing.com

**Sun-Thu noon-11.45pm; Fri-Sat
noon-12.15am**

Born in 1977, neither fire nor the
occasional claim its standards are
slipping have diminished Yang
Sing's reputation for top-notch
Cantonese fare. All things to all
people, an epic dim sum menu
satisfies the lunchtime and shopping
crowd, while the night is given over
to the à la carte dining and fine wine
list. There are even function rooms
and banqueting halls - a scale
reflected in the scope of the menu.
Try a simple yet effective Seafood
dumpling, precisely timed Steamed
scallops or a hearty yet exotic
Braised duckling in spicy yellow
and black bean casserole taken
from those endless banquet menus
(see below). Advice: talk to the Yang
Sing staff, give them a price to work
to and then see what arrives. It's
unlikely you'll be disappointed.

Food 4.5 Service 5 Décor 4

Entertainment: occasional events
(including 'Wok'n'roll' evenings)

Children: very family orientated,
dishes recommended

Vegetarian: vast selection

Set menu: from £16 upwards

Disabled access: full

French

Le Bouchon £B

63 Bridge Street, City

0161 832 9393 4D

Tue-Thu noon-3pm, 5.30pm-10pm; Fri-Sat noon-3pm, 5.30-11pm

Le Bouchon's miniature paintings and lace-swathed tables seem born of another era. Romantic candlelight washes across the Victorian-style room - appropriate for, in movie terms, either a love-charged scene or a melodramatic visitation from 'the other place'. But any spooks around the restaurant leave you alone to enjoy the food. The set menus are good way to get the best of Le Bouchon at a reasonable price. Two courses are £20.95, 3 courses £24.50, which is a bargain. Typical dishes include Fillet steak in Hollandaise sauce or, the star on our visit, Sea bass with scallops and aromatic ribbons of courgette and carrot. Try a dessert too, particularly the La Specialité du Chef - a luxurious crème brûlée with an underlayer of apple crumble served in a tiny terrine. It's a gorgeously toffyish take on British pudding and custard.

Food 4 Service 3.5 Décor 4

Children: smaller portions available on request

Vegetarian: always one main course

Disabled access: partial

Establishment £A

43 Spring Gardens, City

0161 839 6300 6D

Tue-Sat noon-2.30pm, 7pm-10pm

www.establishmentrestaurant.com

The former Lancashire and Yorkshire Bank has an impressive domed interior of plasterwork and marble - shame aout the unfortunate purple intrusion introduced when the building became a restaurant. But the food is much better than this queasy addition. Chef Davey Aspin took over as this book went to press. Dishes he's introduced include Pan fried scallops with braised ox tongue and apple (£12), Duck and foie gras terrine with fig chutney (£11.50) and Pan fried fillets of John Dory wrapped in potatoes with oxtail tortellini and oyster cream (£24). Establishment is expensive, impressive and, food-wise, exciting. It will be interesting to see how it develops under Aspin.

Food 4 Service 3.5 Décor 4

Entertainment: wine tastings, party nights, special events and exclusive uses

Children: smaller portions on request

Set menus: party menus from £30 per head, special Friday dinner menu £22, lunch set menu tbc

Disabled access: full

Francs £B

2 Goose Green, Altrincham

0161 941 3954

www.francs-altrincham.com

Mon-Thu noon-3pm, 6pm-10.30pm; Sun noon-4pm, 7pm-9.30pm

A cheerful and populist restaurant with consistent food quality and warm service standards. If you're with the family and you're in the area then this place is particularly worth a visit. The interior is busy, with rooms occasionally vivid red, occasionally pale, and opening off from each other. Goose Green where Francs is situated is also an oasis from the hoi-polloi crush of a typical Altrincham weekend night. Food examples include Tartalette Marseillaise (£10.50), a vegetable tart with a slice of mozzarella flavoured and served with a salad and rice and Steak du venaison (£14.25), a haunch steak, cooked pink, with a potato rosti and red cabbage.

Food 3 Service 4 Décor 3.5

Entertainment: Fri evenings in the Live Lounge

Children: various menus (one at £6.25 caters for older kids), play area and free baby food

Vegetarian: variety of dishes

Set menu: prix fixe menu £19.50, bon marche menus from £9.95

Disabled access: partial

French

The French Restaurant £A

Midland Hotel, Peter Street, City

0161 236 3333 5F

www.qhotels.co.uk

Mon-Thu 7pm-10.30pm; Fri-Sat 7pm-11pm

The food here is very good, the surroundings opulent yet perversely intimate and the service, led by restaurant boss Bruno Lucchi, impeccable. This place has been a famed locale since its inception in 1903, and was the first hotel restaurant in Britain to gain a Michelin star in the early '70s. The oval dining room is a sweet, mirror-bedecked piece of joyous Roccoco, easily the most stylish of the older dining rooms in the city. The distinguished à la carte menu offers dishes such as a starter of Goats cheese, plum tomatoes, aubergine, caviar with aged balsamic (£10.95) and mains such as Ballontine of salmon with Cornish crab, ravioli and ratatouille of vegetables (£22.95). The French was the 2002 City Life Restaurant of the Year.

Food 4.5 Service 5 Décor 4.5

Entertainment: piano in bar
Set menu: Mon-Thu menu gastronomique, 2/3/4 courses £22/£29/£38
Vegetarian: 3-4
Disabled access: full

Lounge Ten £A

10 Tib Lane, City

0161 834 1331 6D

www.lounge10manchester.co.uk

Tue-Sat noon-2.30pm, 6pm-noon (2am bar licence Fri/Sat)

This is a massive City Life favourite and, as far as we know, unique in the North. It remains the dirty little lush of Manchester restaurants: drunk and giddy on bright reds, faux gilt, saucy candles, mirrors and rude paintings of a Pompeiian orgy. There's even a medium in the unisex toilet. Careful if you take gran though - you might end up munching under a first floor fornication scene. Whilst heterosexual gentlemen might find exiting the second floor private dining room, the Boudoir, a challenge - never has the expression door knob been more appropriate. The food, from chef Marcus Humphrey, is of a high standard, expensive and in smallish portions but worth it if taken as part of the whole Lounge Ten experience. Highlights include the Roast suckling pig (£17.50) with confit potatoes, Savoy cabbage, caramelised apples and chorizo sausage - it also perfectly complements the decadent surroundings. The home-made bread is exceptional. Private hire of the Boudoir (£150, max. 32 seated) makes for a memorable experience for either a few friends and a quiet night or something altogether more extreme - the butler service is a real treat here.

Food 4 Service 4 Décor 5

Entertainment: daily live singers and clairvoyants plus special menus and events on Valentine's etc, including a limousine to chauffeur guests to any bar, club or hotel in the city centre - check website or call for details
Vegetarian: several options

DRINK.   EAT.   RELAX.

THE **BEST** INDIAN RESTAURANT
IN THE NORTH WEST OF ENGLAND
2001, 2002, 2003, 2004 & NOW... **2005**

HI–LIFE DINER'S CLUB

French

Le Mont £A

Urbis, Levels 5&6, Cathedral Gardens, City

0161 605 8282 6B

www.urbis.org.uk

Mon-Fri noon-2.30pm; Mon-Sat 7pm-10.30pm

It would be a strange person who didn't feel a quickening of the blood on first seeing Urbis - a glass slice of modern glamour in the oldest quarter of Manchester. Atop the building, with superb city views, is the equally sharp Le Mont. Here executive chef Robert Kisby is bolstering his already considerable reputation with precise and imaginative French cooking often utilising good North West ingredients. Thus you get Lune Valley venison featuring alongside pure Galloway beef cattle that have been partly reared for Le Mont and heather-fed lamb from the Trough of Bowland, as well as a seasonal menu of regional fresh game. Immaculate presentation is a keynote here too, whether it be a main such as Piece de porc braisé façon Le Mont (£19.95), slow braised belly of pork served crisp with Loch Fyne scallops, black pudding, apple purée and sage

jus or one of the lovely desserts such as Crème légère au cassis, pate d'amande et sorbet cassis (£6.50), light blackcurrant cream stacked with marzipan tuile and with an accompanying sorbet.

Three years on from opening in this challenging but impressive fifth floor site, Kisby puts his success down to, "consistency and quality. We are always aware that we are set apart geographically from the city and we have to make sure we engage with it. Success is built on a regular clientele, and that's only achieved, 99% of the time, by consistent service and food. The best way to build business is by word of mouth before anything else." Yes, minor gripes remain. The biggest problem being that uncompromising design from Ian Simpson Architects, which makes Urbis iconic but not always the most comfortable of buildings.

Food 5 Service 4 Décor 4

Entertainment: occasional events

Children: welcome

Vegetarian: a variety of choices from all sections of the menu

Service charge: 10%

Set menus: 2 course lunch £17.50, 3 course dinner £26.95.

Disabled access: full

Malmaison Brasserie £B/A

Malmaison Hotel, Piccadilly, City

0161 278 1001 9E

www.malmaison.co.uk

Mon-Fri 7am-10am, 6pm-11pm; Sat-Sun 7am-11am, 6pm-11pm

Located in a former textile warehouse from 1904-6, the interior is in an appropriate Art Nouveau style. The result is a foxy, low-lit space that's perfect for intimate tête-à-têtes, whether they're of the romantic or business variety. Also pretty foxy is the cooking from Mark Bennett, who juggles simplicity and sophistication with dishes such as Glazed pork belly (£13.50) with a cheese and onion mash and cider sauce or Lamb culets (£18.50) with grilled artichokes and rosemary. The well-executed Malmaison crème brûlée (£4.95) is a signature dish that interestingly arrives with the recipe in an envelope, and the coffee comes with fluffy chocolate on the side.

Food 4 Service 4 Décor 4

Children: very welcome

Vegetarian: variety

Service charge: 10%

Set menus: lunchtime grand prix menu 2/3 courses, £12.50/£14.50; dinner set menu 2/3 courses, £13.95/£15.95

Disabled access: full

Juniper £A

21 The Downs, Altrincham

0161 929 4008

www.juniper-restaurant.co.uk

Fri-Sat noon-2pm; Tue-Sat 7pm-9.30pm

Ten years old in November 2005 and a marvel of consistency allied to brilliance, Juniper is the only Michelin-starred restaurant in Greater Manchester, and is also winner of the *Good Food Guide* Restaurant of the Year Award 2003 and an AA four-rosette holder. Meanwhile, chef/proprietor Paul Kitching was voted the best chef at the Manchester Food and Drink Festival Awards 2003 and his cooking is adored by both Gordon Ramsay and Heston Blumenthal amongst many others.

The secret to Kitching's success lies in sturdy technical skills and attention to detail, but also in leaps of imagination that more earthbound chefs are simply incapable of. One of the talents of this whirlwind force of nature is to mix unexpected elements in food so cleverly that he not only gets away with it, but succeeds so well that guests have to step outside to allow their senses to recover - well, occasionally. Of course, this Newcastle United mad gentleman needs back-up, so is aided by highly talented kitchen staff and by the astute restaurant management of charming partner Katie O'Brien.

There have been many highlights in the last decade but two particularly notable ones for Kitching were "getting the Michelin star - that's what we opened for and set out to do" and "the moment when the *Guardian* with Mathew Fort gave us an unheard-of 18 out of 20 in a review. We knew we were doing something right then."

A couple of sample dishes from the changing menu might include Butter baked trout filet, glazed lemon tart, goats cheese, barley, hazelnuts, onion glazed, or Saddle of tender Cumbrian venison, long grain rice, leeks, bees pollen, dates, pistachio, tomato, relish and coffee glaze or Classical glazed lemon tart.

The wine list is excellent too, but as a real treat there is a carefully chosen range of ports and sherries - you might want to take one home with you. All in all, Juniper is an epicurean's wet dream.

Of course, this is cutting-edge stuff, so whilst most guests will want to book again as soon as possible, some just don't get it. But the truth is, if you love eating out you're going to have to try Juniper.

A final word from Kitching: "A decade on, everything is rock solid. We're doing good food, but it's personal - it can't really be translated into the mass catering thing. Still, it does occur to me that we need a bigger stage to play on."

More than a hint there that Kitching might be moving his talents away from little Altrincham. Manchester city centre, perhaps?

Please Mr Kitching, pretty please.

Food 5 Service 5 Décor 4

Entertainment: occasional events
Set menus: noon-2.15pm 2/3 courses £17.50/£21.50, surprise lunch 6 courses £40, 8 courses £45; surprise dinner 12 courses £65, 21 tiny courses £101 per head

Le Petit Blanc £B

55 King Street (off Chapel Walks), City

0161 832 1000 6D

www.lepetitblanc.co.uk

Mon-Sat noon-11pm; Sun noon-10.30pm

Le Petit Blanc does some things very well, such as the house speciality Hot smoked salmon with soused beetroot and crème fraiche (£6.50 starter, £13.50 main), the Roast rack of lamb with grilled aubergine and pomme chateau (£16.95), or the home-made ice creams and sorbets (£5.50). Elsewhere, there's less good stuff. You always feel, no matter how many times you revisit, that Le Petit Blanc could be better. This might be unfair - maybe it's the association with that King of Gallic garrulousness, Raymond Blanc, and the feeling that everything should be Le Manoir. In truth, this is a mid-market chain aimed primarily at the business trade, despite very worthy and award-winning attempts to be family friendly.

Food 3 Service 3 Décor 3

Children: children's menu, 2 courses £5.59, 3 courses £7.95
Vegetarian: 3 starters, 2 mains
Set menu: prix fixe 2/3 courses £12/£14.50
Disabled access: full

Dimitris £B

1 Campfield Arcade, City

0161 839 3319 3F

www.dimitris.co.uk

Daily 11am-midnight; bar open until 1am Fri/Sat

A popular place with a lovely arcade to bask under on summer nights. The food starts off being Greek and then goes on an excursion across the whole of the Mediterranean. Tuck into Istanbuli garlic bread (£3.75), which comes covered in a thick layer of rich tomato, or Seafood, lamb or vegetable souvlakias (chargrilled meals with rice, cous cous, salad and sauce) from £8.95. Nothing ever seems to disappoint and some dishes even exceed the cheap and cheerful expectations. And just watching the punters come and go provides value for money. With weekend live music in the bar area on Deansgate plus that continuous buzz throughout the remainder of the restaurant, Dimitris is model of its kind.

Food 3.5 Service 3.5 Décor 3.5

Entertainment: late live music bar Fri, Sat 10pm-1am.
Children: very welcome
Vegetarian: variety of vegetarian and vegan options available
Set menu: variety, eg Mega Mezze £16.35 veg, £19.95 meat or fish

Kosmos £B

248 Wilmslow Road, Fallowfield

0161 225 9106

Mon-Thu 6pm-11.30pm; Fri-Sat 6pm-12.30am; Sun 1pm-11.30pm

Loualla and Stewart Astin's constant inclusion in the *Good Food* and *City Life* guides have given this institution its recognition. Now something of a celebrity, with several TV apearances under her belt, Loualla has left much of the management to her son, Sol. The menu is broad with a good vegetarian input and a choice of chalked-up specials that change nightly. For a starter, try Fasolatha (£3), a soup of cannelloni beans, celery, carrots, tomatoes and olive oil. For mains, try Rosto (£10.50), a dish of lamb shoulder cooked on the bone with onion and cinnamon in a red wine sauce, or Vothino (£10.90), a stew of prime beef with onions, red wine and cinammon. For something sweet, try Bagadoon meh filfar (£4.50), three scoops of vanilla ice cream served on meringue and drizzled with Cyprus orange liquour.

Food 4 Service 4 Décor 3

Children: dishes on request
Vegetarian: wide range
Set menu: many including veg, seafood, meat banquets and set student menu

Indian

Hunter's BBQ £C

94 High Street, City

0161 839 5060 8B

Sun-Thu 11.30am-2am; Fri-Sat 11.30am-3am

Duck, quail, pheasant, rabbit, partridge, venison - who would have predicted that Manchester's best game establishment in 2004 would be a halal Northern Quarter café with 11 stools? The Venison bhuna (say it out loud, it'll make you laugh) is very good, with the distinctive dark flavour of the little bambi coming strongly through the sharp, dry sauce. The meats are charcoal barbecued, which adds an extra quality to the dishes. A full partridge prepared in this way costs £12 - fancy something instead of a turkey this Christmas? Despite the ingredients, none of this is fancy food in the least, nor will it ever win any awards for finesse, but it's great fun. Hunter's opens until 3am on the weekends, so that'd be pheasant madras before even a milkman's stirring.

Food 3 Service 4 Décor 2

Entertainment: a shisha bar upstairs
Children: very welcome, half portions on request.
Vegetarian: several dishes, two different dahl dishes every day
Disabled access: full

Nawaab £B/C £A

1008 Stockport Road, Levenshulme

0161 224 6969

www.nawaab.co.uk

Mon-Thu 5.30pm-11pm; Fri-Sat 5.30pm-11.30pm; Sun 5.30-11pm

Aptly for a restaurant that was a cinema in its previous life, Nawaab is more than capable of stimulating the senses - in this case sight, sound, taste and smell. This place is absolutely huge, with 350 covers on the ground floor alone, which means of course that this isn't the right venue for intimate dining. But with its help-yourself, buffet style, it at least means that you can eat at your own pace amidst the Bollywood photographs. And with a simply bewildering range of Indian starters, mains and deserts to choose from, all as part of the £10 set price, it will satisfy the greediest of Indo-philes without straining the wallet. As a bonus, unlike so much buffet grub, Nawaab keeps things fresh and flavoursome.

Food 3.5 Service 3 Décor 4

Children: welcome
Vegetarian: many
Disabled access: full

Punjab Tandoori Restaurant £B

177 Wilmslow Road, Rusholme

0161 225 2960

Sun-Thu noon-midnight; Fri-Sat noon-1am; Mon 5pm-midnight

This could be just another of the endless Rusholme restaurants, but it makes a case for inclusion here with its devotion to dosas. These South Indian specialities are best described as a foot-long rolled crisped pancake filled with various substantial spicy fillings and two curry accompaniments (for around a fiver). Often eaten as a suppertime dish in southern India, as well as being visually spectacular, they make an addictive meal option or excellent shared starter. But there's good stuff from the north of the subcontinent too, including a variety of sharp and spicy handi dishes. There's an excellent range of vegetarian dishes including dosas with mushroom, potato masala and paneer fillings. For dessert, try Rasmalai - a soft cheese pudding in a milky sauce.

Food 3.5 Service 4 Décor 3

Entertainment: music after 5pm on Fri/Sat.
Children: mild curries, fries etc
Vegetarian: broad range
Set menu: several options

Indian

The Saffron Lounge £B/A

Crown Passages, off Ashley Road, Hale

0161 927 4930

www.thesaffronlounge.co.uk

Tue-Thu 6pm-10pm; Fri-Sat 6pm-10.30pm; Sun 1pm-8pm

Nominated for the *City Life* Manchester Food and Drink Restaurant of the Year 2005. Service is exemplary, with staff willing to explain the menu. A standout starter might be Samundari moti (£8), seared scallop with mustard, curry leaves and coconut milk, and an exceptional main is the Junglee murghi (£14.50), guinea fowl roulade of cottage cheese and spinach in a cashew and caramelised onion sauce. In an age when the choice and variety of cuisine types is almost limitless, many Indian restaurants have realised that to maintain their popularity, they have to modernise. Saffron is an excellent example of this. With a bar added in 2005, this has become a destination venue with sharp looks.

Food 4 Service 4.5 Décor 4

Children: welcome

Vegetarian: many options

Set menu: from £18; Tue-Sun before 6.45pm, there is a three course meal offered at £19

Disabled access: partial

Shere Khan £B

50-52 Wilmslow Road, Rushome

0161 256 2624

www.sherekhan.com

Daily noon-midnight

Shere Khan stands out as Rusholme's most famous curry house, with photos of Noel Gallagher and Vera Duckworth lining the walls. Some of the tables even look out onto the main road, where you can people-watch whilst stuffing your face. There are plenty of generic choices on offer, with the Chicken rogan josh (£5.80) being particularly spicy and tasty, but the Vegetable bhuna (£5.20) is a welcome change from the typical fare with huge helpings of peas and potatoes in the tangy paste. The portions are generously measured too, with side orders of doughy Naan bread and Pilau rice. The Mango lassi (£4.50) is a lovely contrast to the heat elsewhere on the menu. The service is commendable and almost overwhelming at quiet times.

Food 3.5 Service 4 Décor 3

Entertainment: occasional special events

Children: welcome, half portions available

Vegetarian: numerous options

Disabled access: partial

Shimla Pinks £B/A

Crown Square, off Bridge Street, City

0161 831 7099 3D

www.shimlapinksmanchester. com

Mon-Fri noon-3pm; Sun-Thu 6pm-11pm; Fri-Sat 6pm-11.30pm

This is the Indian restaurant as stripped-down stylish retreat - with great washes of contemporary art, low, cubist sofas and not a single Taj Mahal pic in sight. Within Shimla's stylish environs, classical Indian cooking that is as clean and bright as the décor will give your taste buds a slapping. Classical recipes are treated with respect, using fresh herbs and spices, and there's also the occasional nod to new twists and new flavours. Two little beauties *City Life* has enjoyed include the starter of Talley murgh ke pasandey (£4.50), chicken breast marinated with cinnamon, bay leaf, cardomon and cloves before being deep fried, and the Lamb keala molee (£8.45), with roasted and creamed coconut and ground cashews.

Food 4 Service 4 Décor 4

Children: welcome

Vegetarian: many dishes

Set menu: many including lunch tray £7 pp and gourmet banquets from £8.95 pp

Disabled access: partial

うまみ

new fusion restaurant

Open 7 days a week
Monday to Saturday 11am - 11pm. Sunday 12 noon - 10pm
0161 273 2300

OXFORD RD

MANCUNIAN WAY

OXFORD RD

A57 (M)

GROSVENOR ST

scream bar

subway

aquatics centre

umami

BOOTH ST

umami

149/153 oxford rd, manchester M1 7EE

At 11.30am in the morning with the restaurant shutters down, Rusholme is drab. An hour after sunset the same day, it becomes a mini Blackpool, with the illuminations transferred to Manchester for a 365 day run every year.

Down less than a kilometre of Wilmslow Road, visitors will find the largest concentration of Asian (or Pakistani, to be more precise) food outlets in the UK. Just about every one of them seems surmounted by a riot of dancing neon.

Part of the attraction of Rusholme involves window-shopping in the various venues. Those with the mountains of sticky sweets such as the **Sanam Sweet Centre** (0161 224 3852) can't help but attract your attention, along with the multitudinous array of menus outside the restaurants with their individual nuances, influences and styles.

The choice includes award-winning big wigs like the **Darbar** (0161 224 4394), the intriguing, often magical (it has a magician) **Lal Haweli** (0161 248 9700) and the **Royal Naz** (0161 256 1060). You might also want to try the **New Tabak** (0161 257 3890), the **Dildar** (0161 248 8880), **Hanaan** (0161 256 4786) and **Sangam** (0161 257 3922). There's even a specialist ice-cream outlet, **Moonlight**, serving desserts and drinks like the memorable Faludas and Lassis.

In fact, for those feeling nostalgic for travel in the Subcontinent of Asia, an evening stroll through Rusholme, breathing in those smells of charred tandoori ovens, roasting spices, onions and garlic glistening with ghee and simmering sauces, can be a therapeutic experience.

It's not just the restaurants either - many of the other outlets boost the mood too, such as the sari shops, book and video stores, greengrocers with outdoor displays as big as tennis courts (or so it seems) and jewellers gleaming with gold.

Rusholme

Curry glossary

These definitions come from the superb handbook 'Rochdale's Curry Quarter' produced by the Rochdale Partnership. This is available free from the Tourist Information Centre (01706 356 592) and gives details of the Milkstone Road area of the town with history, background and listings from the Asia Restaurant to the Kamran Sweet Centre.

Aloo: Potato.

Balti: A balti dish is basically the same as a karahi - a wok-shaped cooking pan with two ring handles, which comes in all sizes, including small ones with a wooden stand for serving individual portions at your table. Balti or karahi cooking involves stir frying quickly over a high heat on the stove top. The name originates in the mountains of Baltisan in Kashmir.

Bhindi: Okra, also known as 'ladies fingers'.

Bhuna: A sautée paste, dryer than a curry sauce.

Biryani: A fruit-and-nut rice dish with vegetables, meat or fish, garnished with an omelette and served with the curry sauce of your choice.

Chapatis: Sometimes called 'roti'. Wholewheat flour is used to make pancake-shaped, unleavened bread.

Curry: The word comes from the Tamil 'kari'.

Dal: Lentils and other pulses, usually cooked with spices. There are about 60 different pulses available in India and Pakistan - check out the variety in cash and carries.

Dahnsak: A sweet but piquant dish of Persian origin with lentils, pineapple and tomatoes.

Dopiaza: Literally 'double onions', so there will certainly be onions involved.

Northern Quarter 8B/C

Rusholme is always noted as the curry centre of Manchester but those who enjoy a more café style of eaterie should take in a few of the little curry houses in the Northern Quarter. Daily specials are cheap, cheerful and at times easily as good as those down on the 'curry mile', certainly more consistent at the moment. But remember this is basic market food, the daily dishes that serve many of the local community that work in the rag trade and other businesses in town. The surroundings are basic but that's beside the point because for around £4 for lunch you've got yourself a tasty bargain. One of the hardest to find is **This'n'That** (3 Soap Street, off Thomas Street) – if you can find this place you deserve a reward, but then again if you've found it you've already got your reward. Another favourite is **The Yadgar** (Thomas Street) with good naans and a friendly service. Other recommendations include **Al-Faisal** (58 Thomas Street), and **Kabana** (52 Back Turner Street). Whichever you choose these remain the best Sunday morning hangover cures in the world.

Ghee: Clarified butter. A substitute made from vegetable oil is also available, and keeps longer.

Gobi: Cauliflower.

Gosht: Meat, invariably lamb.

Jalfrezi: Cooked with onions, peppers, garlic and ginger.

Karela: 'Bitter gourd', a knobbly green vegetable.

Keema: Minced meat.

Kofta: Spicy meatball.

Korma: A mild curry with nuts and cream.

Lassi: A chilled yoghurt drink either salted or sweetened. Mango lassi is a delicious sweet version.

Masala: A masala will usually include cream, almonds and extra spices.

Mughlai: A reference to the Mogul courts of a bygone era, this usually means a mild dish using yoghurt, traditionally flavoured with exotic spices such as saffron.

Murghi: Chicken.

Naan: This bread is made with special flour, yeast, eggs, milk and sugar, and can be griddle cooked or cooked in a tandoor. As well as plain naan, there are several more elaborate versions: kema naan (stuffed with mince), peshwari naan (stuffed with almonds and fruit) and kulcha naan (sprinkled with sesame seeds).

Pakora: Potatoes, flour, onion and spices, deep fried, sometimes served by weight. Other variations include mixed vegetables and chicken versions.

Palak: Spinach.

Paneer: Cheese curd.

Paratha: May be a circle of layered flaky pastry or a thicker fried version of the chapati. Can be stuffed with minced meat or vegetables.

Pulao rice: Spiced rice fried in ghee, often brightly coloured.

Rogan josh: Cooked with tomatoes, pimentoes and onions.

Sag: Spinach.

Samber: A sharp aromatic spice mix originally from south India.

Seekh kebabs: Sausage shaped, made with minced lamb, skewer cooked and strongly spiced.

Shami kebabs: Usually burger shaped, made with mince, flour and spices and deep fried.

Tandoor: Clay charcoal-burning oven used for cooking breads and meat at searingly high temperatures.

Tikka: Usually chicken or lamb cubes marinated in yoghurt and cooked on a skewer over a charcoal grill.

Vindaloo: A highly spiced and hot curry, originally from Goa.

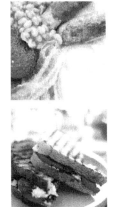

Café Paradiso £B

Alias Rossetti Hotel, 107 Piccadilly, City

0161 247 7744 9D

www.aliashotels.com

Mon-Thu until 10pm; Fri-Sat until 10.30pm; Sun until 5pm

Under new chef David Gale, who was nominated for Manchester Food and Drink Festival Chef of the Year in 2005, Café Paradiso's upmarket British cuisine is winning favour across the North West. The trio of Grilled lamb liver and kidneys (£13) is a fortifying treat, whilst the Seabass (£13.50) showcases a rare talent for cooking fish. Starters offer inspiring twists on convention: Scallops, for example, are paired with braised beef (£5.95) and Parma ham with pomegranate (£5/7). The menu rotates regularly and the wine list cherry-picks a range of global wines. Unfortunately, the cuisine is occasionally let down by amateurish service. Still there's a lot of creativity at work here and the Bring Me Food menu introduced in 2005 is a wonderful way of serving with every course a suprise courtesy of the chef.

Food 4 Service 3 Décor 4

Children: smaller portions
Vegetarian: variety
Set menu: Bring Me Food menu £24 per head, the chef selects starters and mains
Disabled access: full

Croma £C

1 Clarence Street, City

0161 237 9799 6D

www.croma.biz

Mon-Sat noon-11pm; Sun noon-10.30pm

The website reads 'Croma - Manchester, Boston, Chorlton'. That's Boston, Massachusetts, and Chorlton-cum-Hardy. What do you mean they're not really compatible? Croma is that type of business, local and quirky, but still the best indie pizzeria in town for service, style and product. The city centre building is smart on the outside and located in a fabulous position just off Albert Square (we've yet to be given the budget for a Boston review and the Chorlton place opens just after this book appears on bookshelves). The menu is simple and cheap but with enough choice to provide solutions for most diners. A range of dishes might include Garlic bread with tomato and basil (£2.25), Peking duck pizza (£7.20), Chicken Caesar salad pizza (£6.95) or Sticky toffee pudding (£3.95). The service stands out for its care and warmth.

Food 4 Service 4.5 Décor 4

Children: separate menu such as small lasagne or small margarita/ham/mushrooms plus ice cream and soft drink £4.95
Vegetarian: more than 15
Disabled access: partial

Est Est Est £B

5 Ridgefield, City

0161 833 9400 5D

www.estestest.co.uk

Mon-Wed noon-10.30pm; Thu noon-11pm; Fri-Sat noon-11.30pm; Sun noon-10pm

Well-appointed Italian restaurant, part of the locally devised chain Est, Est, Est. Clever and consistent in usually well-designed settings the restaurants are undergoing gradual refurbishment to update them. The pizzas are decent and there is a good à la carte. A selection might include Anti pasto caldo (to share, £9.95), the Chicken primavera (£11.75), a house speciality of chicken breast, crushed new potatoes, julienne of spring veg and white wine cream sauce, and the Choux bombe (£3.75), Italian style choux pastry filled with Belgian white chocolate ice cream and topped with warm choc sauce. Service is 99% of the time superb and a bonus for families - real efforts are made with children. Also at Didsbury, Knutsford and elsewhere.

Food 3.5 Service 4 Décor 4

Children: £5.95 for lasagne / spaghetti bolognese / chicken escalopes / make your own pizza, ice-cream, drink
Vegetarian: wide choice
Vegetarian: extensive choice
Disabled access: full

...enjoy 20% discount with our pre-theatre offer (3-6pm), please quote 'City Life Food and Drink Guide offer'

east 東海

East Restaurant is getting rave reviews...

52-54 FAULKNER STREET MANCHESTER M1 4FH
TELEPHONE 0161 236 1188
FAX: 0161 2283833

Palmiro £B/A

Upper Chorlton Road,
Whalley Range

0161 860 7330

www.palmiro.net

**Mon-Sat 6pm-10.30pm; Sun
noon-10.30pm**

Palmiro has always been stylish,
from the font of its name to the sharp
interior lifted by the red photographic
artwork. A planned refurb and
extension in spring 2006 will ensure
this remains the case. Fortunately,
the food needs no reworking.
"I want Palmiro to be based on
substance," says proprietor Stefano
Bagnoli. "With the new space, we'll
have the chance to offer a drink
to people waiting for tables and
make the place more comfortable,
but we'll always be a restaurant
first and foremost." Too true. One
dish from the seasonally changing

à la carte menu blew us away:
the Parma stuffed lamb loin chops
with pistachio crust (£15.75) was a
work of beauty, showing balance,
flair and exquisite handling. Don't
miss puds such as the Roast figs
and honey ice cream (£3.95) either.
The care shown also applies to the
wine list, which Bagnoli confidently
calls the "best Italian list in the
North West". Possibly so. There
are occasional inconsistencies, but
Palmiro generally delivers attractive
and gutsy modern Italian food
- described as one of the ten best
Italian restaurants around in the
Times. If you hit this place right you
just have to agree.

Food 4.5 Service 3.5 Décor 3

Children: small portions, meals on
request
Vegetarian: a variety
Set menu: Sunday lunch menu.
Disabled access: full

Felicini £B

749 Wilmslow Road,
Didsbury

0161 445 2055

www.felicini.co.uk

**Mon-Sat noon-11pm 11am-
10pm; Sun noon-10.30pm.**

Part of the same group as the
excellent city centre Grinch see
British section above, this remains
a lively restaurant that attracts a
young and young at heart crowd.
The menu is dominated by pizza
and pasta dishes with an authentic
Tuscan twist – Felicini has one of
the best award-winning training
programmes around which includes
Italian site visits. New menu delights
include Conchiglioni (£7.97) with
smoked salmon, asparagus, capers
and mascarpone, Panzerotto
(£5.95), rolled stuffed pizza, sliced
to share with goats cheese and
sunblush tomato and Braised lamb
shank (12.95) with chorizo and
mixed italian bean cassoulet. There
are sister Felicinis in Monton (0161
789 2675) and Wilmslow (01625
529 0524).

Food 4 Service 4 Décor 4

Children: smaller portions
Vegetarian: a selection of starters
and mains
Set menus: for parties over 8. Two
options £20 or a £25 3 course
meal

Italian

Olive Press £B

4 Lloyd Street, City

0161 832 9090 4E

www.heathcotes.co.uk

**Mon-Thu 11.45am-10pm;
Fri-Sat 11.45am-11pm; Sun
noon-9pm**

Part of the Heathcotes empire, the
ambition here is to emulate the
success of nearby Piccolino. It's not
achieved that (nobody has), but it
has triumphed in providing superior
Italian comfort food in easy-going,
attractive surroundings. Natural light
streams in from north and south via
big sash windows, the floor is by
turn tiled or laminated, the woodwork
is bright and images of fruit-laden
plants reinforce the mood - the place
could have been designed by a
committee of Sunday supplement
lifestyle editors with Tuscan second
homes. There are seasonal menus
including all the classic pizza and
pasta dishes as well as some less
usual fare such as Casserole of
baked cod and mussels (£15) with
tomatoes, new potatoes and chorizo.
The bar area is good place for a
drink throughout its opening times.

Food 3.5 Service 4 Décor 4

Entertainment: live jazz every Wed
and last Sun from 7pm
Children: menu from £3 - 25p
from every order goes to Childline
Vegetarian: several options
Disabled access: full

Piccolino £B

89 Clarence Street, City

0161 835 9860 6D

**Mon-Sat 10am-11pm; Sun noon-
10pm**

Exceptionally popular city centre
rendezvous that has many
aficionados, including large
numbers of VIPs (the head of City
Council events thinks "this is the
best restaurant in the world" - which
may be going too far). It's smart too,
with big view-the-world windows,
wooden panelling and sharp,
design-led furnishings. The staples
of Italian cooking are covered in
a straightforward, unpretentious
way, covering the bases from pasta
and pizzas through to favourites
including the Crostini con fegato
(£4.95), sauteed chicken livers,
grapes, Marsala wine and pine
kernels, and Costata de bue con
patate (£14.50), chargrilled and
marinated rib of beef with garlic and
rosemary potatoes. There is good
live crooning on Sundays when the
atmosphere is very laid back. Piccs
is also good for a coffee break.
Winner of the Manchester Food and
Festival Family Friendly 2005 Award.

Food 4 Service 4 Décor 4

Entertainment: live jazz music Sun
1pm-4pm
Children: families very welcome
Vegetarian: several
Disabled access: partial.

Ramsons £A

18 Market Place,
Ramsbottom

01706 825070

www.ramsons.org.uk

**Wed-Sat noon-2.30, 7pm-
9.30pm; Sun 1pm-3.30pm**

This is a gem of a restaurant run by
the eccentric Chris Johnson, who
sees food as one of the genuine
sensual experiences. He would
love us to eat more slowly, allowing
ourselves the time to savour our
food. His particular love is the
flavour of Piedmonte and Liguria in
Northern Italy, and Italian methods
of cooking are his inspiration.
There is also a strong commitment
to using the very best in regional
foods. If you want to splash out,
try out the superb-tasting menu
with nine courses. Dish examples
might include Rare rib eye of
Bowland beef (£19.50) with pioppini
mushroom sauce and tiny jacket
potatoes or Wild blackberry soufflé
(£7.50) with fragolina grape sorbet.
Superior wine selection.

Food 4.5 Service 4 Décor 4

Children: well-behaved children
allowed
Vegetarian: several
Set menu: several including chef's
tasting menu (£47.50) and Sunday
lunch 2/3/4 courses £19.50/
£23.50/£27.50
Disabled access: partial

Italian

San Carlo £B/A

King's Street West, City
0161 834 6226 4D
Daily noon-11pm

An immediate hit when it arrived in the city in 2004, San Carlo is an up-scale Italian chain - although don't mention that particular C-word in the place, as they want to stress the individual qualities of restaurants in places such as Bristol, Leicester and Birmingham. The interior is as bright and brisk as the buzzy ambience, with pride of place given to the open kitchen with its huge copper and wood stove. Whether it's actually as good as all those people think is another matter, as it can be a little hit or miss. Food-wise, there's a full à la carte menu, but also a chalkboard from which guests can choose an array of market-fresh fish and seafood. Interesting dishes include Carpaccio tascano al porcini (£6.95), marinated Tuscan beef in extra virgin olive oil with porcini and topped with flakes of parmesan cheese or Salmon ravioli romanov (£9.85), ravioli filled with salmon, flambeed in vodka with pink peppercorn, a touch of tomato sauce and cream.

Food 3.5 Service 4 Décor 4

Entertainment: occasional
Children: welcome, smaller portions available
Vegetarian: options available
Disabled access: full

Stock £A/B

4 Norfolk Street, City
0161 839 6644 6C
www.stockrestaurant.co.uk
Mon-Sat noon-10pm

This is one of those restaurants in Manchester that you have to visit. Run by former Manchester Food and Drink Festival Chef of the Year Enzo Mauro and family, Stock is frequently cited as one of the best Italian restaurants in the UK. Famous for its food and its award-winning wine list, the site is no less impressive, lying as it does in Manchester's domed and Edwardian former Stock Exchange. In fact, through imagination and solid technical skill, using home-made foods and market-fresh veg, the Mauros have created a temple to Italian cuisine out of a temple to Mammon. Dishes combine classics with regional tastes and innovative modern cooking. Examples are

Bruschetta di fegatini di pollo picante (£6.50), devilled chicken livers served on a walnut brushetta, and Pulcino marinato al limone e dragoncello (£16), poussin marinated with tarragon and lemon, pan-fried and with a beetroot and fennel salad. Enzo's way with fish and seafood is well known and the Seafood platter is recommended. There's a comprehensive range of Italian cheeses and hams which has to be seen to be believed. With memorable dinners whether for one or fifty, Stock is one of the best choices for gourmet group food as well.

Food 4.5 Service 4 Décor 4.5

Entertainment: jazz on Fri, opera and other theme nights, tastings
Children: smaller portions
Set menu: table d'hote 2/3 courses £12.80/£15.80, plus buffet and lunchtime 'rapido' menus
Vegetarian: several pasta and other options
Disabled access: full

Italian - Japan

San Marino £B

Belmont Road, Bromley Croft, Bolton

01204 811 206

Mon-Sat noon-3pm, 5pm-10.30pm; Sun noon-10.30pm

Hidden in the hills between Bolton and Manchester, San Marino is a charmer of a restaurant twinkling tastily for those who know where to look. For locals and non-locals alike, it's worth the detour to this former pub for the garlic bread alone. There are no sticky white baguettes for the chefs here - rather flatbreads are layered with dripped slices of tender aubergine and garlic cloves, or dusted with herbs. Seafood glistens across the menu from starters like king prawns, oysters and kalimari through to meaty chargrilled fillets of sea bass as a main course. The risotto is another must-try. Alone or as an accompaniment to lamb kebabs, its sublime, jammy flavours satisfy both appetite and senses. Portions are on the sturdy side and the wine list is varied, with a rightful focus on Mediterrenean grapes.

Food 4 Service 4 Décor 3

Entertainment: occasional

Children: welcome, smaller portions available

Vegetarian: options available

Set menus: call ahead

Disabled access: full

New Samsi £B/A

36-38 Whitworth Street, City

0161 279 0022 8F

www.samsi.co.uk

Mon-Fri noon-3pm, 6pm-11pm; Sat noon-midnight; Sun noon-4.30pm, 6pm-11pm

There's never been a Japanese food revolution in the city, so we're reduced to few places to choose from. Still, we could do worse than New Samsi, which offers a good introduction to the mysterious East. Take the beautifully presented Mixed sushi course (£11), for instance, and you'll find your own Fujiyama of flavours. The Shichimi never disappoints too, especially the fierce black tiger prawn example (£10.95). More exotic fare includes the Unagi (£9.95) - glazed eel on rice. The latest initiative is Samsi Express, a shop in the basement where you can buy all the ingredients to make your own delights either at home or in the restaurant upstairs. For a small surcharge, diners can buy their nori seaweed, sushi rice and other essentials and then make full use of the facilities. The shop also sells a selection of reasonably priced gifts.

Food 4 Service 3 Décor 4

Children: menu £4.50

Vegetarian: several options

Set menus: various from £6.50, eg Sumo Wrestlers Feast (£26.50)

Teppanyaki £B/A

58-60 George Street, City

0161 228 2219 7E

Mon-Fri noon-2pm; Mon-Sat 6pm-11pm

If you're feeling brave and sociable as well as hungry, this flashy Japanese restaurant provides a unique dining experience. Six to twelve diners are seated around a steel hotplate where a personal chef creates your meal from scratch, beginning the show with a blast of the furnace and a flourish of their big, sharp knife. The menu is pricey but varied and wholesome, and the benefits to watching your meal being made are amazing entertainment (often verging on performance art - our chef re-enacted the Ashes victory with egg shells) and seeing everything that goes into a dish - simply, well-prepared, perfectly cooked fresh vegetables, meat and fish, with herbs and spices. Specialities include Spicy stir-fried lamb with spring onion and ginger (£15.15) and King prawns and jumbo scallops cooked in Tokyo butter sauce (£16.45).

Food 4.5 Service 4 Décor 4

Entertainment: the chefs!

Children: share adult portions

Vegetarian: 3, plus set menu

Set menus: 6 from £22-£35. 2 course lunch £10. Pre-theatre dinner 3 courses before 6.30pm

Kosher - Korean - Middle Eastern

Kosher

A good place to go kosher food hunting is Kings Road. Here you'll find the excellent Deli King, the friendly Ashers restaurant and the more formal JS restaurant (0161 798 7776). This latter provides a wide variety of quality kosher classics from across the Diaspora and makes for a good destination restaurant. Ashers (0161 773 1414) is more informal, a cosy pale yellow, tiled venue with a very amiable eponymous proprietor. Food is schizophrenic, with Middle Eastern and Mediterranean influences, thus you'll find tasty Morrocan fish balls and the Ashers special pizza. Another recommended kosher venue is Pagoda, Bury Old Road (0161 798 4149). For a kosher deli, see the Food Shopping section.

Koreana £B

40a King Street West, City

0161 832 4330 4D

www.koreana.co.uk

Mon-Fri noon-2.30pm, 6.30pm-10.30pm (Fri 11pm); Sat 5.30pm-11pm

This long-standing favourite has been serving traditional, colourful Korean food for 20 years. The emphasis at Koreana is on meals served simply, by knowledgeable staff keen for you to navigate your way through the menu without a hitch. Perhaps the best and easiest way to accomplish this is to opt for Koreana's banquets (£15): offering at least a couple of choices at each stage. Alternatively, try their Kun Mandoo fried dumplings (£4.50), stuffed with spicy beef and vegetables followed perhaps by Beef bulgogi (£6.50), a classic Korean marinade of garlic, soy and sesame. Vegetarians should try Gugsu bokum (£6.50), wok-fried egg noodles stir fried with vegetables and soy. If you're in a rush, the Koreana lunch boxes provide some of the best takeaways in town - the medium priced £4 offer is enough for two.

Food 4.5 Service 4 Décor 3

Children: meals on request
Vegetarian: 5 starters and 8/9 mains plus veg banquet
Set menu: various and banquets

Aladdin £C

529 Wilmslow Road, Withington

0161 434 8558

www.aladdin.org.uk

Mon-Fri 5pm-11pm; Sat 2pm-11pm

If you're aware that this won the snappily titled Manchester Food and Drink Festival Best Provision for Vegetarians 2005 Award, you might be surprised to find that it sells meat as well. Still, the accolade is deserved for the variety of veg on offer, not that it looks that way on entering, as access to the first floor restaurant is via the kebab shop below. Up here, the food can be exquisite, and includes endless hot and cold starters such as pastries, vegetarian dips, tabbouleh salads and mains of charcoal-grilled veg, meat and fish. Good veggie stuff includes rice pot dishes such as the Ful medamas (£3.50), dry foul (fava) beans with pitta bread, cooked and mixed with tomatoes, garlic, herbs and onions, or Mujaddara (£3.50), rice, lentils, veg oil and lentils. Don't miss the Muhalbeh (£2), milk pudding served with pistachio nuts and seasoning, either. Aladdin is unlicensed, so bring your own bottle.

Food 4 Service 3 Décor 2

Children: welcome, lots of suitable starters
Vegetarian: many options

Middle Eastern

The Cedar Tree Lebanese Restaurant £C

69 Thomas Street, City

0161 834 5016 8C

Mon-Sat noon-10pm

Passers-by could be forgiven for thinking the Cedar Tree a cheap takeaway. Inside, it's a mess of fluorescent lighting, white tiles and functional tables, complete with insane water feature. But hold your fast food judgement, because the nosh is worth risking the abuse of your aesthetics. Unmissable highlights include the Tabbouleh and the Falafel rings, the first an authentic combination of crushed coriander, flat-leaf parsley and tomatoes zinging across the palate with hardly any wheat to drag its natural vibrancy down, the second a team of sesame-encrusted delights continents away from the usual balls of chickpea stodge. Try also the Kafta khashkhash - lamb kebabs in a tender tomato sauce, which perfectly complements the side of Bazinjan al-rahib - dripping grilled aubergines on a bed of lettuce, garlic and lemon. Unlicensed but bring your own bottle.

Food 4 Service 3 Décor 1

Children: welcome
Vegetarian: several interesting options
Disabled access: partial

The Persian Grill £C

Barlow Moor Road (opp. Southern Cemetery), Chorlton

0161 860 6864

Mon-Tue noon-10.30pm; Thu-Fri noon-11pm; Sat 4pm-11pm; Sun 1pm-10pm

Persia Grill, almost anonymous from the outside, combines good service with simple food cooked well. The tiny interior is filled with heavy wooden furniture, kilim, flowers and Persian figures of antiquity and legend. The naans made from fresh dough on the premises might be some of the best you've ever tasted - they should be part of legend too. The mint leaf with paneer (goats or sheeps cheese) comes as a free appetiser and works a treat. Mains include Shishleek (£7.95), lamb chops in saffron, Zoreshk polo (£5.95), half a chicken with rice and berries, and the House special (£7.95), a mix of lamb shish kebab. The chops and the chicken kebabs come in large portions with colourful assaults of flavour. As for the tea (50p), mingled with spices and herbs via a samovar, it is wholeheartedly recommended. Unlicensed but bring your own.

Food 4 Service 5 Décor 4

Children: made to feel welcome and kitchen will be flexible with choice
Vegetarian: several dishes

Petra Restaurant £C/B

Upper Brook Street, Victoria Park

0161 274 4441

www.petra2eat.co.uk

Daily 5pm-11pm; Mon-Fri 11.30am-2.30pm; Sat-Sun 1pm-11pm

Related to Aladdin (see opposite), this is more up-to-date version. Artwork and photographs around the walls, even the delicate wood and metal latticework of the ceilings, let you know that care and attention is paramount to the whole experience. And the same treatment has been lavished on the food. Combining incredible value with good flavours, Petra is a good option in this part of under-restaurented Manchester. Recommendations include Fatayer (£3), pastry stuffed with spinach, onions, parsley, pomegranate sauce and herbs and deep fried, and Tubakh rawhou (£7.50), lamb with aubergines, courgettes, garlic herbs and so on. You can take home a doggy bag if you can't finish. Unlicensed but bring your own bottle.

Food 4 Service 4.5 Décor 3.5

Children: welcome
Vegetarian: many options
Disabled access: partial

Modern European

Flamin' Nosh £B

97 Stamford Street,
Stalybridge

0161 338 5555

www.flaminnosh.co.uk

**Mon-Fri noon-2pm, 5pm-10pm;
Sat 3.30pm-10.30pm; Sun
2.30pm-9.30pm**

Sister restaurant to Hyde's Stables
Bistro, the fun red, yellow and
orange interior of this western-
themed restaurant - ideal for kids
and kidults alike - belies an easy
simplicity in both the presentation
and execution of the food. A giant
stone cave oven dominates the
open kitchen and gives the part
Tex-Mex, part modern British
menu flavour and texture. Staple
starters such as Deep-fried Cajun
mushrooms and their own wonderful
Flamin' dough balls (both £4) are
unfussy, flavoursome and delivered
with just the right amount of bite.
Ditto the main of Aromatic duck
pizza (£7.85), a wonderful mass of
topping, crisp base and doughy
centre also available to take away,
and the huge Chicken fajita (£11.95)
- all big enough to stop John Wayne
himself in his tracks.

Food 4 Service 5 Décor 4

Entertainment: occasional
Children: ideal for kids
Vegetarian: wide selection
Set menu: Meal Deal £17.95
Disabled access: full

Idaho £B/C

Manchester Road, Chorlton

0161 881 6699

www.idahobar.co.uk

**Mon-Sat 6pm-11pm; Sun 6pm-
10.30pm**

A titchy split-level restaurant in cool
blue with a couple of tricks up its
US/world inspired sleeve. First off,
the food is decent standard at spot-
on prices. Signature dishes include
Sausage with lentils and chilli butter
(vegetarian option too, both £7.50),
which is damn fine and sports an
excellent tough mash potato and
that vigorous butter. Then there's the
Blackened tuna with green rice and
salad (£8.50), Vegetarian enchiladas
(£6.75) and a specials board. For
afters, try an obligatory home-made
Pecan pie (£3.50) amongst others.
The second trick and treat is the
drinks selection, which includes a
mind numbingly massive selection
of around 100 world beers with the
odd surprise cider. There are five
draught beers too, including a good
pale ale, Anchor Steam (£2.65),
from US micro Sierra Nevada and
wines from Latin America, Oregon,
Canada, Washington State and -
unsurprisingly - Idaho.

Food 3.5 Service 4 Décor 3

Children: good family welcome and
smaller portions
Vegetarian: third of the menu
Disabled access: partial

Opus One £A

Radisson Edwardian Hotel,
Peter Street, City

0161 835 9929 5E

www.radissonedwardian.com

Daily noon-3pm, 6pm-11pm

Opus One sits within the five-star
Radisson Edwardian's splendid
remodelling of Edward Walters'
superb 1856 Free Trade Hall. If
arches are your thing then this
has the best set in the North,
with half the Peter Street arcade
now encased in glass to allow
magnificent viewing of the wildlife
out there on a Saturday night. Away
from the arches, it's all black lacquer
effect, red seats and rings of red
neon around the pillars - sort of hit
and miss Art Deco. The bar is a
glitzy place for schmoozing with the
well-heeled and occasional celebrity
guest. Sample dishes include
Organic salmon with hazelnuts,
spinach and a white lemon butter
sauce (£15.50) or Roasted guinea
fowl with haggis and charlotte
potatoes (£16.50). In truth, though,
Opus One has yet to make any sort
of mark on the Manchester food
scene.

Food 3 Service 3 Décor 3

Entertainment: occasional
Children: menu
Vegetarian: menu.
Service charge: 10% (12.5%)
Disabled access: full

Modern European - Nepalese

The Second Floor Restaurant, Bar and Brasserie £A/B

Harvey Nichols, 21 New Cathedral Street, City

0161 828 8898 5B

www.harveynichols.com

Mon-Sat 10am-10.30pm; Sun 10am-6pm

The Restaurant has views across Exchange Square and the hoi polloi at leisure and offers upscale à la carte food such as Classic veal 'Houstain', buttered spinach, soft fried egg and port jus (£9.50). The Brasserie is the venue for ladies who lunch with smaller bites such as Smoked haddock crostini, tomato, pickled onion and rocket (£10.75). Food comes from the very capable Robert Craggs and is invariably of a good standard. But, and it's a big but, the service can let the place down, usually by being so unhurried as to be comatose. Still, the venue looks the part - check out that marvellous pin cushion effect on the bar - and the cocktails are superb.

Food 4 Service 3 Décor 4

Entertainment: film nights, tastings
Children: flexible with dishes
Vegetarian: several options
Service charge: 10%
Set menus: Tue-Sat 6pm-10.30pm
2/3 courses £11.50/£14.50
Disabled access: full

Thirty Nine Steps £B

39 South King Street, City

0161 833 2432 5D

Mon-Sat noon-2.30pm, 6pm-10.30pm

Though its sister restaurant in Styal might be physically more attractive destination than this, the original, Thirty Nine Steps is nevertheless a Mancunian institution that is well worth a visit. Focusing on market-fresh French and Italian cuisine, the space is intimate, discreet and rather understated - although this year, *City Life* noted that it could do with a lick of paint in places. An ever-changing menu means each visit is a unique experience, and we really enjoyed the unfussy Noisette of lamb (£17.95) on our last visit, though vegetarian options were a little thin on the ground. The wine list is small but well chosen, taking in a comprehensive cross-section of tastes and regions in pursuit of variety. What sets the Thirty Nine Steps apart from many restaurants in the city is its understated classicism in both ingredients and presentation. It's expensive, sure, but without any hint of ostentation. A unique dining experience.

Food 3 Service 4 Décor 3

Children: smaller portions
Entertainment: occasional events
Vegetarian: 2 dishes at time of visit

Great Kathmandu £C/B

140 Burton Road, West Didsbury

0161 434 6413

www.greatkathmandu.com

Daily noon-2.30pm, 6pm-midnight

From the outside, this Nepalese restaurant looks as though it's been transported straight from the set of *Only Fools And Horses*. The chintzy décor certainly gives the place a warm, retro feel. But in terms of service and menu choice, it's very much up to speed with today's demands. There's a great selection of vegetarian dishes as well as chef's house specials. The mixed starter with a variety of beef, lamb, chicken and prawns is perfect for two (£8.50). And a main of Chara masala (£5.50) has just enough ginger and garlic to prevent the chicken being too spicy for non-seasoned palates. A welcoming family restaurant, Great Kathmandu is certainly an added charm in Burton Road's collection of quality restaurants.

Food 4 Service 3.5 Décor 2

Children: very welcome
Vegetarian: several options
Set menu: 3 courses and coffee for £10.25
Disabled access: partial

Café Lloyd

Superb Traditional Fish & Chips

HOT SPECIALS
BREAKFASTS
SANDWICHES

Eat in or Take Away

Open 7:30 - 3pm

Easy access through Lincoln Square Situated between Albert Square and Deansgate

0161 835 2073

16 Lloyd St, Manchester

Modern European

The River Restaurant £A

Lowry Hotel, Dearman's Place, off Chapel Street, City

0161 827 4000 4C

www.thelowryhotel.com

Mon-Sat noon-2.30pm, 6.30pm-10.30pm; Sun 12.30pm-3.30pm, 7.30pm-10pm

The River Restaurant (originally the River Room) opened at the Lowry Hotel in 2001 with a rotten egg of an idea. To impress the yokels, company bigwigs gave the restaurant a silly association with Marco Pierre White. Punters weren't stupid, of course - they knew that White was an absentee chef. Now with Eyck Zimmer in control of the kitchens, the River Restaurant has finally emerged from the long shadow of that foolish start. This man can cook. Okay, the menu varies seasonally, but take

the starter *City Life* enjoyed: the Caramelised lamb sweetbreads with caper and raisin chutney (£10.50). This provided meat that had a vivid, light flavour and the gentlest of consistencies whilst the chutney was a revelation. Similarly, the main of Roast squab pigeon with summer cabbage and onion fennel marmalade (£22.50) was a triumph. Lots of chefs, after showing off with the starters, fall away at second base, but not Zimmer. Full marks for presentation - an uncrowded plate, appealingly arranged with good colours - and full marks for the combination of the foods, which were effortlessly balanced. The desserts showed the same attention to detail. The Creamed rice pudding with English marmalade (£7) bore the same assured technique of the other courses: clarity in the flavours yet a rewarding complexity too. With a superior wine list, the only problem lies with the décor, which is

still sub-airport waiting lounge. That aside, with Zimmer at the helm the River Restaurant has become one of the leaders in Mancunian dining. It provides a fine up-market evening or lunchtime out whilst each course gives you a thrill of expectation. If Zimmer can keep this up, the place will become a destination for the whole of the North of England and then way beyond. If you can't afford it right now, miss out on the next three visits to lesser restaurants and save up for a night out here.

Food 5 Service 4.5 Décor 3

Entertainment: pianist and singer Thu-Sat 7.30pm-10.30pm, Sun 1pm-3.30pm

Children: welcome

Vegetarians: separate menu

Service charge: 10%

Set menus: lunch 2/3 courses £13.50/£14.50, dinner 2/3 courses £18.50/£20.50

Disabled access: full

Gurkha Grill £C

198 Burton Road, West Didsbury

0161 445 3461/5444

www.gurkhagrill.com

Sun-Thu 6pm-midnight; Fri-Sat 6pm-1am

Another justifiably popular stalwart of the West Didsbury eating out scene. Here the food is saturated with lots of unusual Nepalese specialities plus familiar Indian fare too. The Prawn sandeko (£5.95) starter is generous enough for two to share: cooked simply in green chillies and coriander, it's very hot and fresh. A signature dish is Chicken sandeko (£5.95), chicken breasts cooked in a clay oven and cubed with chilli, coriander and garlic. Or try the Aloo chat (£2): spuds in appetising mustard seed sauce. Gurkhali (£6.25) with chicken, lamb, prawn or veg comes highly recommended, the spicy, tomato-based curry with green chilli permeating the flesh of the various meats. Very good for vegetarians.

Food 4 Service 3 Décor 3

Entertainment: occasional including culture programmes

Children: dishes on request

Vegetarian: 2 set menus and plenty of dishes

Set menus: from £11.95 (vegan option) up to £59.95 (meat for 4 people sharing)

Disabled access: partial

New Himalayas £B/C

945 Stockport Road, Levenshulme

0161 248 8882

Daily 5pm-midnight

The New Himalayas remains at the dizzy heights of Nepalese cuisine - or at least at base camp. Dig into to whatever you fancy and you won't be disappointed. Try the finely presented Kaira dhaniye ka paneer tikka (£2.75), cubes of paneer (goats or sheep cheese) marinated with crushed mangos, coriander, a touch of chilli and chopped mint leaves. Peak with Chicken Himalya (£7.50): breast of chicken stuffed with mince and cooked in creamy coconut sauce. A signature dish is Tikhey jinghey (£8.95), king prawns in tomatoes, onion, capsicum and garlic. If you have an appetite the size of Everest, the chef will prepare such speciality dishes as the Barra, a whole young lamb stuffed with tilda, rich herbs, nuts and spices, at 24 hours notice (cost per head).

Food 3.5 Service 4 Décor 3

Children: on request

Vegetarian: separate menu

Set menus: 4, with prices starting at £12.95 per person

Disabled access: full

Cachumba £B/C

220 Burton Road, West Didsbury

0161 445 2479

www.cachumba.co.uk

Mon-Sat 6pm-10pm

Slightly out of place within the world of West Didsbury dining, Cachumba sits in the midst of Burton Road's eateries like an experimental teenager, with a taste for all things South East Asian. If they have a signature, it's probably the juicy Javanese fish curry (£), which blends the subtle flavours of white fish with fresh tomato, coconut and lime leaf. The Thai king prawns (£) are presented in a sharply sweet Thai basil, red chilli and lemongrass sauce and are eminently recommended. There's even an awesome Sticky toffee pudding (£) to incongruously round things off. With fine food, good value and a warm atmosphere, Cachumba, nominated for the *City Life* Restaurant of the Year 2003, isn't part of the young professional clique of restaurants - rather it asserts its own identity in an individual manner, setting an example to all the smaller businesses.

Food 3 Service 2.5 Décor 3

Children: flexible with dishes

Vegetarian: 9 options

Pan-Asian

Pacific £B

58-60 George Street, City

0161 228 6668 7E

www.pacificrestaurant.co.uk

Daily noon-11.30pm

After a fire and a rebuilding period, Pacific has returned to somewhere near the form it enjoyed in 1999 when it became *City Life* Manchester Food and Drink Festival Newcomer of the Year. It is still split into two floors of contemporary chic, the upper serving Thai food and the lower Chinese. Chef's specials upstairs include Primrose sharks fin (£38) and Steamed whole eel with garlic and black bean sauce (£12 per lb). Downstairs, highlights include Baked English crab with dry yellow curry or glass noodles (£8 per lb) and Steamed whole sea bass Thai style with lime leaf, lemon juice and chilli pepper (£16 per lb). The menu may differ slightly each season and each cuisine has its own kitchen, chefs and waiting staff.

Food 4 Service 4 Décor 4

Children: adapt dishes to suit
Vegetarian: many
Service charge: 10%
Set menu: three banquets from £20.50-£35.50 per person.
Disabled access: full

Pan Asia £B

Faulkner Street, City

0161 236 6868 7E

www.pan-asia.co.uk

Mon-Sat noon-late

Blues and oranges predominate in this basement restaurant that stands out with its odd, even perverse, design. For example, the various TV screens broadcast Eastern channels replete with game shows and soaps, then there are lightboxes cut into the walls filled with everything from toys to terracotta warriors. The food can, on occasion, be as memorable, covering all bases between Chinese, Japanese, Thai, Malaysian and Vietnamese. Starting at the bottom, the lunchtime buffets at £6.95 are some of the best around, neither stodgy nor dating from the Triassic period. Off the à la carte, try Mixed seafood tempura (£6) for delicacy, the Chicken in coconut shell (£8) or the Beef with black pepper sauce in a crusted bread dome (£8) for something more substantial. There's a decent range of juices too, but why tap water costs 50p is beyond reason.

Food 3.5 Service 3 Décor 3.5

Children: will adapt dishes to suit
Vegetarian: many
Service charge: 10%
Set menu: Mon-Fri buffet from £6.95 per person

Tampopo £C

16 Albert Square, City

0161 819 1966 5E

www.tampopo.co.uk

Mon-Sat noon-11pm; Sun noon-10pm

Simplicity always wins out in the end and this restaurant is an object lesson in how to create a beloved brand by doing the easy things exceptionally well. The airy basement restaurant displays classic Japanese influences with the bench seating and tables. There's a minimalist look about the place too, lightened by a changing display of progressive artworks. All the stalwarts are present and correct, from Nasi goreng (fried rice, £7.75-£8.75), via Tempura vegetables (£3.95) to Pad Thai (fried noodles, £7.50-£8.50). The Ramens (noodle soups from £6.75) come from heaven via the images on a perfect silkscreen - we're trying to say they're art. Get stuck in if you can. Tampopo has spread from Manchester to Leeds, the Trafford Centre and London.

Food 4 Service 4 Décor 4

Children: separate children's menu
Vegetarian: many options including vegan
Set menus: Backpacker £13.95 3 courses; Eastern Odyssey £16.95; Express £6.75 noon-7pm

Pan-Asian - Philippino - Seafood

Wagamama £C

Spinningfield Square, City

0161 833 9883 4D

www.wagamama.com

Mon-Sat noon-11pm; Sun 12.30pm-10pm

Wagamama provides fusion without confusion. It's bright, simple, efficient, tasty and to many people very familiar. Manchester may already have one of these Far East fusion kitchens in the bosom of the Printworks (Corporation Street, City, 0161 839 5916 7B), but more of the same is welcome. Their new, brighter home is set on the glassy ground floor of the soaring new Royal Bank of Scotland building. Get stuck in to Chicken gyoza (£4.25), five little dumpling mouthfuls of heaven, accompanied by a chilli, garlic and soy sauce combo, or Ginger chicken udon (£7), chunky noodles infused with fresh coriander, snow peas, red onion, bean sprouts, chilli and pickled ginger, and you won't be disappointed. There's good puds to be had too, although these owe more to grandma's trad recipes than anything from Japan.

Food 3.5 Service 4 Décor 4

Children: yes, £2.75-£3.75
Vegetarian: huge choice
Set menu: Absolute (chicken) £11.25, Pure (vegetarian) £11 and Complete (fish) £12, 2 courses plus drink.
Disabled access: full

Cora's Philippino Restaurant £C/B

174 Oldham Road, Ashton-under-Lyne

0161 330 4978

Mon-Tue 9am-3pm; Thu-Sat 9am-3pm, 7pm-10pm; Sun 9am-4.30

Deep in the suburbs of Ashton-under-Lyme there resides a café/restaurant that can at the very least be described as unique. Originally a tearoom set up by Cora - an émigré from the Philippines who came to the UK to learn catering in the '70s - it's little more than a converted shop, but what delights lie within this strange little curiosity. During the day, it is a tearoom serving cakes and sandwiches, but by night dishes such as milk fish and Lumpia (a Philippino spring roll) take pride of place. Surely there's no other similar establishment in the North West? It's worth phoning ahead if you're not local, as the first time *City Life* went to review the place, the front door was locked on an 'open' evening and Cora was happily singing karaoke to herself inside. Bless.

Food 4 Service 3 Décor 2

Children: welcome
Vegetarian: separate menu

Livebait £B

22 Lloyd Street, Albert Square, City

0161 817 4110 5E

www.santeonline.co.uk

Mon-Fri noon-10.30pm; Sat noon-11pm: Sun noon-9pm

For some reason, Livebait changed from an exclusively fish and seafood policy a couple of years ago to one that was watered down (or beefed up) with a few crowd-pleasing meat dishes. Which is a shame, but there's still enough here to please the lovers of briny beasts. Take the Classic platter (£28.50 for one, £49.50 for two): this has more than enough Whitby crab, Madagascan crevettes, tiger prawns, Atlantic prawns, rock oysters, mussels, cockles and clams to keep most people happy. In fact. the joy of seafood is exactly that - the rending and ripping, opening and digging to reveal and consume the precious flesh within. The interior is brisk with tile and chrome and there's a superior kids menu.

Food 4 Service 3 Décor 4

Entertainment: occasional music
Children: welcome, very good menu £5.95
Vegetarian: two or three choices
Service charge: 10%
Set menus: 2 courses £12.95, 3 courses £16.50
Disabled access: partial

Manchester Food & Drink Festival 2005

Winners and nominees (city centre unless stated)

City Life Restaurant of the Year
Winner: The Market Restaurant

Juniper (Altrincham), Isinglass (Urmston), Café Paradiso, Saffron Lounge (Hale), Stock

City Life Bar of the Year
Winner: Bluu

Bar Fringe, Centro, Knott Bar, Panacea, Socio Rehab

City Life Coffee Shop of the Year
Winner: Suburb

Cornerhouse, Baileys (Ramsbottom), Manchester Art Gallery Café, Oklahoma, Zest

City Life Pub of the Year
Winner: The Kings Arms (Salford)

The Church (Saddleworth), The Hare and Hounds, The Lamb (Eccles), Stalybridge Buffet Bar (go on, guess), Ye Olde Man and Scythe (Bolton)

City Life Newcomer of the Year
Winner: Marmalade

Dilli (Altrincham), Fat Loaf (Ashton-on-Mersey), Lotus Bar and Dim Sum, Marmalade (Chorlton), Northern Quarter Bar and Restaurant, Persia Grill (Chorlton), Soup Kitchen

Chef of the Year
Winner: Lisa Walker, Isinglass (Urmston)

David Gale, Café Paradiso; Mike Harrison, formerly at Chefs at Paragon (Bolton); Paul Kitching, Juniper (Altrincham); Simon Rimmer, Greens (West Didsbury); Ian Morgan, formerly of the Establishment

Family Friendly Venue
Winner: Piccolino

Croma, Manchester Art Gallery, Oca (Sale), Olive Press, Sweet Mandarin

Best Retail Outlet
Winner: Hymans aka 'Titanic'

Katsouris, Harvey Nichols, Red House Farm (Dunham Massey), Unicorn Grocery (Chorlton), Winos (Oldham)

Best Vegetarian
Winner: Aladdin

Greens (West Didsbury), Idaho (Chorlton), Isinglass (Urmston), Market Restaurant, Petra (Longsight)

Simon Rimmer of Greens: Restaurant of the Year 2004

Outstanding contribution: Iain Donald

Chef Iain Donald's influence on the Mancunian restaurant scene began when he became the operations director of the locally based Est Est Est group. The restaurant's take on modern Italian cuisine was refreshing and the King Street flagship restaurant was one of the busiest operations in the city. Its success was largely based on Donald's attitude to running restaurants, a mantra that has since become his catchphrase: 'Fanatical attention to detail' (imagine it being said, with every letter emphasised, in a slightly intimidating Scottish accent).

Eventually the owners of Est Est Est sold up and turned to Piccolino and the Restaurant Bar and Grill. The first thing they did was to re-recruit Donald to the team. Although the ownership of the company has changed, its continued success is staggering and is testament to the tight rein that Donald keeps on the operations, his keen eye for what goes out of the kitchen, and the loyalty and commitment he inspires amongst his staff. The group now has the thriving city centre Panacea bar as well.

Another key characteristic is his deep commitment to training. He has inspired a whole generation of budding Manchester chefs and restaurateurs who have gained experience, knowledge, and the occasional Fergie-style 'hair dryer treatment' under him. He currently works closely with the award-winning catering department of South Trafford College, offering placements to their students.

Evuna £B

277-9 Deansgate, City

0161 819 2752 4F

Mon-Sat 11am-11pm

www.evuna.co.uk

One of the outstanding wine restaurants in the North and a tough, handsome, little number in brick and timber. Appropriately the shelves are filled with enough bottles of Spanish wine-making excellence to make Bacchus weep for joy. Foodwise, you can munch on classic tapas such as Rape con pimenton (£6.95), fillet of monkfish with paprika, and Potage de chorizo con garbanzos (£6.25). There are also large platters to share based on meat (£18.95), fish (£19.95) and vegetables (£15.95). The house signature is Pescados a la sal (£15.95): seabass baked in rock salt with seasonal vegetables. The defining characteristic, as it should

be with the best Spanish fare, is one of substance - more Sancho Panza than Don Quixote, reality before fantasy. Food aside, it's the selection of 600 plus Spanish wines, from £4 a glass to bottles at £1,600, that makes Evuna an essential visit. These can be bought in bottles and cases and taken home - Evuna is an off-licence too. If you're staying in, the wine is decanted and then poured, little by little, into glasses larger than the aquariums at Manchester University. A good example would be the smooth but rich Melqiour from Rioja (£20 / £12 take-way). A gorgeous white might the Missenyora from Catalonia (£20/ £10, exclusive like the Melquior to Evuna), a dry, crisp delight. Sherry is represented with six well-chosen examples from wafer-dry to the hedonistically sweet version from the Pedro Ximinez grape (£39.99/ £19.50). There's a good selection of

Spanish spirits including Fundador brandy to put punters in mind of staying up in Ibiza til 7am on spirit-fuelled binges.

Food 4 Service 4 Décor 4

Entertainment: wine tastings, occasional music

Children: welcome

Vegetarian: tapas, paellas and tarrinas

Set menu: several

Disabled access: partial

Spanish - Thai

El Rincon de Rafa £B

Longworth Street (off Deansgate), City

0161 839 8819 4E

Mon-Sat noon-midnight; Sun noon-11pm

Popular, filled with the buzz of chatter and hard to get into on weekend nights, El Rincon de Rafa is a long-standing favourite in the city and comes closer to any other restaurant to capturing the true flavour of bar/eaterie in, say, Burgos or Segovia. It's also one of the hardest restaurants to find in Manchester, stuck down a back alley off Deansgate. Owned by an ex-Stockport County playing Spaniard - try to spot his picture on the wall - the place is popular during the first half of the week and packed at weekends, so book ahead. There is a huge selection of tapas including Muslitos de cangrejo (£3.95), crab claws, classic Tortilla Espanola (£3.35), Champinones cabrales (£4.50), mushrooms and blue stilton. There are also distinguished main dishes such as Paellas (2 people for £8.75).

Food 4 Service 4 Décor 4

Children: tapas are perfect for kids - try Albondigas

Vegetarian: 8 tapas, 1 main, soups and salads

La Casona £B

27 Shaw Road, Heaton Moor

0161 442 5383

Mon-Sat 5.45pm-11pm; Sun 1pm-10pm

Recent visits confirm how lucky the Heatons are in having this excellent, atmospheric and warm award-winning establishment. Asturian mountain man Carlos Menedez is proprietor and oft-time chef. This gent provides a clue as to how an independent restaurant should be led: he is a visible presence not only conducting the kitchen but, when time allows, visiting the tables for a chat and a laugh. Good quality tapas are available - the perfect child's food, of course, consisting of tasty but not overwhelming morsels. There are mains too, including the Pixin a la cazuela, an Asturian dish in an earthen bowl of monkfish, prawns and mussels in a tasty sauce with chilli heat. Another earthenware delight is Gambas al ajillo, king prawns cooked in garlic and olive oil and brought to the table sizzling hot.

Food 3.5 Service 5 Décor 4

Children: menu plus tapas, children eat free on Sundays

Set menus: tapas banquet, bread, salad £8.95; parties menu £14.95

Vegetarian: around 15 choices

Disabled access: partial

Koh Samui £B

16 Princess Street, City

0161 237 9511 6E

www.kohsamuirestaurant.co.uk

Mon-Fri noon-3pm; daily 5.30pm-11.30pm

City Life remembers eating in this basement restaurant when Thai food was still a rarity to all but the Thai people and lemongrass meant something instead of an excuse for planting the word Thai on any old rubbish. Koh Samui's starters are always a highlight of a meal that cuts both ways from an experience point of view. Recently the Chicken in pandanus leaf (£5.95) and Pan fried crispy oysters (£6.95) left us with little room to enjoy the mains. The traditional green, yellow and red curries (£7.45-£9.45, ingredients depending) should not be avoided because the subtlety of tastes is mesmerising. It's very much an occasional restaurant (though business lunchtime offers are a good options, noon-3pm), but the helpful staff will guide you through the large menu - and warn you not to eat the pandanus grass.

Food 4 Service 3 Décor 3.5

Children: welcome

Vegetarian: 22 dishes

Set menus: for 2 £25-£30, for 4 £20-£35

Siam Orchid/ Orchid Lounge £B

52-54 Portland Street, City

0161 236 1388 7E

Mon-Fri noon-2.30pm, 5pm-11.30pm; Sat-Sun 5pm-11.30pm

A complete night out under one roof, this quirky Thai establishment comprises a karaoke bar, the Orchid Lounge, above a colourful restaurant. You can order food on both floors, with the Lounge also offering buffets for parties. Why not warm up with some of Manchester's tiniest and crispiest Vegetable spring rolls (£3.80)? - 'Nobody Does It Better'. Next up, a Spicy Thai salad (around £5) - 'Killing Me Softly' - with just the right amount of heat. Follow this, if you dare, with a traditional Red curry (£6.95) – 'I Will Survive'? Or if you're not quite that confident in public, how about Garlic and lemon poached fish broth (£12.50) - 'Eel Meat Again' - with a portion of delicate Steamed coconut rice (£2.50) - 'I've Got a Lovely Bunch of Coconuts' - to complete your set.

Food 3.5 Service 4 Décor 4

Entertainment: occasional musical entertainment, karaoke upstairs
Children: menu on request
Vegetarian: separate menu
Set menus: 2 courses from £18-£25, banquets from £17-£27, main courses half price at lunchtime
Disabled access: partial

Thai-E-Sarn £C

210 Burton Road, West Didsbury

0161 445 5200

www.thai-esarn.co.uk

Mon 6pm-11.30pm; Tue-Fri noon-2.30pm, 6pm-11.30pm; Sat-Sun 6pm-11.30pm

Amongst the bourgeois dining of West Didsbury, this is the loose cannon. A love of Elvis dictates everything from the décor and the background music to the karaoke slots and the 'Love Me Tender' chicken parcels. But somehow, it's not tacky. The unassuming and polite waiting staff, in traditional Thai dress, set a sophisticated tone. An extensive menu, with plenty of vegetarian choices, can leave you spoilt for choice. Som tam (£5.95) is a fiery way to begin things with green papaya and herb tomatoes that have an addictive chilli kick. Excelling in curries, the Goong pad prik king (£9.95) is a green curry with thick juicy prawns and crunchy vegetables. With mains accompanied by their gravity-defying sticky rice, there's sometimes no room for pudding. By the end of the meal, with a bulging belly and a head full of song, you'll feel a new affinity towards the King.

Food 4 Service 4 Décor 3.5

Entertainment: karaoke
Vegetarian: 19 choices
Disabled access: full

Café Istanbul £B

79 Bridge Street, City

0161 833 9942 4D

www.cafeistanbul.co.uk

Mon-Thu noon-11pm; Fri-Sat noon-11.30pm; Sun 5.30pm-10pm

You can't go wrong with Cafe Istanbul: it looks smart, provides good quality food at reasonable prices and makes its guests feel comfortable. Which is why it's usually busy. The menu is appealing, offering hot starters such as the Minced lamb meatballs (£3.90). There are good mains too, City Life favourites being the Oven baked lamb in fresh tomato and herb sauce (£12.80) and the Chargrilled seafood feast (£13.90 per person, minimum of 2), which comes on a silver platter with swordfish, halibut steak, king prawns, rice and mixed salad. A signature dish is Aubergine lamb, lean meat slowly cooked in red wine and served on a bed of aubergine pureé (£12.30).

Food 4 Service 4 Décor 4

Children: ask for advice, flexible
Vegetarian: many
Set menus: lunch menu £7.95, lunch combos £4.50-£5.75, theatre menu 5.30pm-7pm, 10pm-11pm £9.95
Disabled access: full

Turkish Delight

Barlow Moor Road, Chorlton

0161 881 0503

Mon-Fri noon-2.30pm; Mon-Sun 5pm-11pm

This wonderful Chorlton institution will have had a complete refit by the time the next issue of *City Life Food & Drink* comes along, transforming the intimate family-run take-away/ restaurant to take in a bar where people can enjoy a drink and mezes along with the exhaustive menu. In the meantime, enjoy a wide selection of grilled meat and fish dishes cooked by friendly chefs in what's effectively the charming back room of a great take-away. Being a take-away, of course, the place is constantly buzzing with life, which makes the Turkish Delight the perfect place to discreetly people-watch. The Karisik izgara (lamb, chicken, spiced kebab, £10.95) is a wonderful dish that might defeat all but the most ravenous meat eater, concentrating on meat and spice over sauces. In that respect, the dishes are largely very pure. Last time *City Life* visited this perennial fave, we left all recommendations to the chef who came up trumps on every level, including a choice of Turkish wines.

Food 4 Service 4 Décor 3

Children: welcome
Vegetarian: many dishes
Disabled access: partial

Earth £C

16-20 Turner Street, City

0161 834 1996 8C

www.earthcafe.co.uk

Tue-Sat 10am-5pm

Earth is part of the Buddhist Centre, so is a place of peace and contemplation. It is decorated in a simple, minimalist style but there's nothing cold about the atmosphere - especially in the snug poetry corner. The service is canteen style, with the emphasis on mixing and matching from a menu that is different and fresh every day. The Chef's special (£5.90) combination of a main, side dish and two salads offers a well-balanced meal and great value for money. And the jacket potatoes are cooked to fluffy perfection. Of particular note are the juices, smoothies and shakes. The invigorating Hey Jude (£2.80 300ml, £3.30 400ml) orange, apple and ginger smoothie is named after that other smoothie, Jude Law, who filmed that dreadful version of *Alfie* nearby in 2004.

Food 4 Service 4 Décor 4

Entertainment: occasional photography and painting exhibitions
Children: very welcome
Disabled access: partial

Eighth Day £C

111 Oxford Road, University

0161 273 1850

www.eighth-day.co.uk

Mon-Sat 9.30am-7.30pm

Now with a complete facelift and make-over, this venerable institution looks set for many years to come. The shop space has been expanded, organic fruit and vegetables have been introduced to the shelves and, crucially, the café has moved downstairs to a newly inserted basement. Eighth Day serves two home-made soups every day (£2.10), two fresh stews (£3.65) and a selection of bakes (£4.50), plus Veggie burgers (£4.75) and Falafels (£4.75). Breakfast is always a good deal too: Veggie house breakfast (£4.95), Sausages on toast (£2.25), Two sausages and beans on toast (£2.80), Scrambled egg on toast (£1.85) and Beans on toast (£1.85). For those who want to have a go themselves, the *Eight Day Cookbook* is an unfailing helpmate in the kitchen.

Food 3.5 Service 3 Décor 3

Entertainment: annual celebration of Vegan Week, Sep/Oct, plus occasional guest speakers on nutrition
Children: welcome
Disabled access: full

Vegetarian

Greens £B

43 Lapwing Lane, West
Didsbury

0161 434 4259

**Tue-Fri noon-2pm, 5.30pm-
10.30pm; Mon and Sat 5.30pm-
10.30pm; Sun 12.30pm-3.30pm**

Nowadays you find that vegetarians
quite often look like perfectly normal
people, and it's a tribute to this fact
that restaurants like Greens exist.
Since winning *City Life* Restaurant
of the Year 2004, Greens continues
to serve serious food in stylish
surroundings, acknowledging
that veggies don't all want to
eat vegetable lasagne or goats
cheese every time they dine out.

Interestingly, Simon Rimmer and
Simon Connolly, who set up the
restaurant 15 years ago, are both
carnivores, and perhaps this is
reflected in the wide appeal of their
food. There are no obvious meat
substitutes on the menu - apart
from the home-made Cheshire
cheese, mozzarella and herb
sausages, served with mustard
mash, Boddington's gravy and
sweet-and-sour beetroot (£10.50),
and the obvious nod to Chinese
crispy duck in the Deep-fried
oyster mushrooms, pancakes
and plum sauce (£5.25) starter.
But all dishes are highly inventive
and beautifully presented, with a
broad enough range to appeal to

most palates. The Spinach and
Blacksticks blue roulade with fresh
tomato ratatouille salad (£10.50) is
a particularly well-rounded assault
of flavours and textures. Add some
super-friendly service and calming,
uncluttered décor, and it's easy to
see why Greens ranks with the best,
regardless of its meat-free focus.
The perfect place to treat yourself
or your local veggie to a taste of the
new, unrestricted high life. A winner
in 2004 but a winner everytime.

Food 4.5 Service 4 Décor 3

Children: menu, all dishes £4.25
including free ice-lolly
Set menus: 3 courses £14.95,
5.30pm-7pm Tue-Fri, all Sun, Mon
night
Disabled access: partial

Vegetarian

The Greenhouse
£C

331 Great Western Street, Rusholme

0161 224 0730

www.dineveggie.com

Daily 6.30-late; Sun noon-3pm

God bless the stalwarts of the world, who soldier on in a world of change. God bless the Greenhouse for being a beacon of eccentricity in an increasingly homogeneous world. With green-painted exterior, fairy lighting and a location amidst terraced streets, the Greenhouse has become the well-loved, old aunt of Manchester vegetarianism, delighting and bemusing veggies and vegans alike for 22 years. Whatever your predilection, it will cater for it, from fake meat dishes such as Sweet potato goulash and dairy product courses such as heavy Savoury cheesecake to the plentiful vegan menu including a non-meat Haggis. If that wasn't enough, all the portions are huge, come with lots of salad and never rise above £8.45. The extensive drinks menu is supplemented by a list of fruit wines.

Food 3.5 Service 3 Décor 3

Children: welcome, many starters are like small mains
Set menu: Valentine/Christmas menus
Disabled access: partial

Vegetarian Society

Manchester is a long established veggie-friendly city, as the movement began here in 1809, inspired by a local preacher Rev William Cowherd who preached on abstinence of the flesh.

Perhaps the continuing prominence of the movement is a testament to the work of the Vegetarian Society, still based here in Altrincham. This registered charity is the oldest vegetarian organisation in the world and offers advice, recipes and information on the vegetarian lifestyle. Their website (www.vegsoc.org) receives more than 18,500 hits each month and the Cordon Vert cookery course pages are among the pages most regularly visited.

The charity's registered trademark, the 'Seedling Symbol' (launched in 1969), has come to be regarded the world over as a trusted stamp of vegetarian approval and is only awarded to those products that are free of animal flesh, meat or bone stock, animal carcass fats, gelatine, aspic or any other products resulting from slaughter. Approved products will only contain free-range eggs, not be tested on animals or contain GMO ingredients. The society is currently seeking to get the term 'vegetarian' defined by law, so that food described as vegetarian meets with the society's definition.

The society's recipe booklet, 'Festive Fantastic', offers a choice of Cordon Vert Christmas dishes such as Winter walnut and mushroom rolls or Christmas crostini. Or for those hoping to make vegetarianism a New Year's resolution, they have produced 'Food for Thought' - a supportive seven-step-guide to staying veggie, as well as delicious recipes.

The Vegetarian Society can be contacted at Parkdale, Dunham Road, Altrincham WA16 4QG (0161 925 2000) - a friendly, informative response is guaranteed.

Getting High

The most interesting food and drink street in the North

Okay, it doesn't really look like this. This is a Playmobil version of High Street 8A from clever Manchester design agency Dinosaur. But it shows **Bluu** (pg 106) and **Hunter's** (pg 15). The first of these is the *City Life* Manchester Food and Drink Festival Bar of the Year 2005 and the second the nuttiest curry café in the known world. Off picture on High Street you'll also find the **Market Restaurant** (pg 27), the *City Life* Manchester Food and Drink Festival Restaurant of the Year 2005, Chinese restaurant **Sweet Mandarin** (pg 20), margaritas bar **Rodeo** (pg 102), sassy and sexy cocktail trendsetter Socio Rehab (pg 116) and the very handsome **Northern Quarter Restaurant and Bar** (pg 18). Meanwhile **Oklahoma** (pg 142), the most eccentric coffee shop you'll ever encounter lies a little way south down the street as does the **English Lounge** (pg 130) pub. Just off High Street lies the delightful **Odd Bar** (pg 102), the **Bay Horse** (pg 101) with its red pool table and the best selection of teas you could wish to find in the **Chinese Arts Centre** (pg 142) caff. One of the best traditional pubs in the city lies two minutes away, the **Hare and Hounds** (pg 125), with its Wednesday night sing-a-long.

Is there anywhere in Europe where in such a short stretch of pavement you get such a curious and joyous variety of venues? From fine dining to fast food, from the trendiest drinks to the most traditional pubs, it's all here. This is why this illustration is perfect for High Street, capturing something of its special charisma.

The seven deadly sins of manchester food and drink

Eating and drinking are two of the fundamentals of life. We can avoid art, sport, music and work if we're lucky or very clever. We can even avoid sex, if we want. But we can't avoid food and drink. This essential pair, as well as keeping us alive, also directly engage four of our senses: taste, smell, touch and sight. They can even disable the fifth - hearing bacon crackle in the morning and the pop of a cork from a bottle can make us weak at the knees. Food and drink are necessity and pleasure, survival and sensuality.

But love of food and drink can become a pursuit in its own right. Far removed from the need for nutrition, it can become a passion, a hobby, an absolute obsession. The scholars of the world's religions don't like obsession - unless it's with their own icons and dogmas, of course. That's why the seven deadly sins - here comes the lightning bolt - can be such fun. These are the Manchester venues in which to lapse into sins - some are built for pleasure, some divine retribution. Why not indulge in your own deadly food and drink festival.

Lust
It's got to be Lounge Ten (Tib Lane, City centre, 834 1331). Where else can you get soft porn on the walls whilst eating? It's even more graphic in the private dining area, including a painting of eating on the walls that has nothing to do with nourishment and a doorknob that heterosexual men may find hard to use. Oh madam, those veins.

Gluttony
Gorge yourself at **Gaucho Bar and Grill** (St Mary's Street, off Deansgate, City centre, 833 4333). Get the Lomita de cuadril, a 950-gram monster steak the size of Denmark, which costs £38 and is intended for two people to share. Eat it yourself. Afterwards, you can visit Nawaab (Stockport Road, Levenshulme, 224 6969) - a restaurant bigger than Belgium - and get one of the lovely help-yourself buffets for a tenner.

Sloth
There's only one place to go. Under Tribeca (Sackville Street, City centre, 236 8300) is **BED**. Here you can eat your food, take your drinks, nod off, even occasionally sing karaoke literally lying down. Sloth is a sin of

waste. To really get into the part, visit a McDonald's or Burger King, or stay at home and watch a cookery programme.

Avarice
Who are the most overpaid, pampered people in the city? Find avarice where Premiership football players gather, which would be the **Living Room, Sugar Lounge** and **Panacea**. Find Rio or Wayne, stroke their hair and say, "It must be very difficult". Combine the result with anger below or envy just after that.

Wrath
Squares, Walkabout, Sports Café, Edwards - take your pick on a Friday or Saturday night when some of our least worthy citizens come to do battle. Real bon viveurs never fight - they merely sigh and reach for another cognac. Anger can be induced as well by inappropriate service charges - this can happen most notably at **Zinc** (Triangle, City centre, 827 4200) with its unacceptable 12.5% stealth tax.

Envy
Visit **Juniper** (The Downs, Altrincham, 929 4008) and get green eyed at the flavours that Paul Kitching produces. Why can't we all cook like this and think these things up? Saddle of tender Cumbrian venison, long grain rice, leeks, bees pollen, dates, pistachio, tomato relish, beetroot, coffee glaze - how does he get away with it?

Pride
Get the table at the prow of the sixth floor at **Le Mont** (Urbis, City centre, 605 8282) and observe the pathetic, scurrying masses below. Here in this glass tower, you're better than that - you're above all them. Take a sip from your Louis Roederer Cristal (£225 a bottle), laugh at the people on the big wheel and roll a piece of marizipan tuile round your mouth.

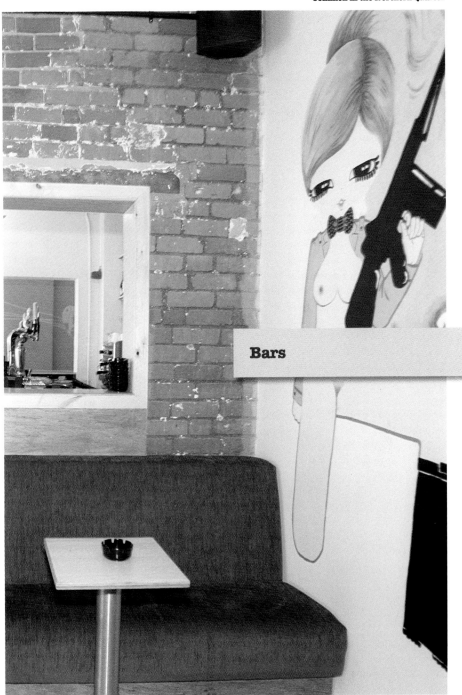

Bars

Panacea

Bars intro

Bars can be either depressing or invigorating - they rarely occupy any middle ground. Unlike pubs, which have tradition behind them, bars need to create a sense of anticipation to make any impression. Manchester is fortunate for the number and variety of good bars it possesses. Most of these are independent, such as Odd, Knott Bar, Sand Bar and Socio Rehab, and most are maverick rather than mainstream. And with the arrival of spectacular Panacea bar, Manchester showed it could go glam too.

In the last few years, several good chains have also joined the party. Indeed, Bluu, part of the Fat Cat group, is this year's *City Life* Manchester Food and Drink Festival Bar of the Year.

As usual, it remains a puzzle as to the exact definition of a bar. Several bars provide very good food, such as the Bar, Velvet and Zinc, all three of which would have fitted in the restaurants section of this book. Meanwhile, some bars are part of a shared venture with restaurants, thus Obsidian, Choice, Dimitris and others.

PLEASE NOTE

Alcohol licensing laws change in November 2005. The opening times that venues have given in this section may radically change also. Some bars have yet to decide how late to pursue trade from November. Please call ahead to avoid disappointment.

The Bay Horse

The Bay Horse

35-37 Thomas Street, City

0161 661 1041 8B

www.thebayhorsepub.co.uk

Mon-Sat noon-11pm; Sun noon-10.30pm

This place demonstrates the difficulty of defining what is a bar and what is a pub by being a bit of both: an old pub with a buzzy, creative atmosphere associated with the more chi-chi type of venue. The interior shows this straight off, with a wild scatter of chaise longues, wall settees, upright chairs, artworks and a rich arts and crafts wallpaper. Downstairs it's crazier, with an insane red pool table and a lunatic mannikin dressed like a window laydee from Amsterdam plus rude images in the toilets. Food wise, there's nothing but nibbles, so it's all about drinks and that funky atmosphere.

Entertainment: pool table, DJs every weekend from 8pm, open mic night every other Wednesday

House special: buy a bottle of house wine for £6 Mon-Fri 5pm-7pm

Disabled access: partial

Common

Edge Street, City

0161 832 9243 9B

Mon-Wed 5pm-midnight; Thu-Sat 5pm-2am

This takes the DIY ethic to the extreme, with felt, chipboard and furniture that might look more at home in your garden. The artwork applied directly onto the walls, like some sort of internalised street art, adds a striking and frequently changing dimension. If you get the idea straight away, you'll love the place. If you don't, you will be wondering when Common will ever get finished - perhaps it's better to consider it a work in progress. Still, for a lot of local aficionados, this might be a venue made in heaven or, as it could be, straight out of New York's newly cool Williamsburg or even East Berlin. Whatever, it's canny, funny and an unintimidating addition to the Northern Quarter. In fact, you might say this type of venue is exactly what this corner of the city is all about.

Entertainment: DJs

House special: Hoegaarden

Disabled access: partial

New Bars

Odd

Mojo

Back Bridge Street, City

0161 839 5330 4D

Mon-Sat noon-2am; Sun 5pm-12.30am

Mojo rocked Leeds when it opened and still attracts rave reviews. But Mojo Manchester (opening as this book goes to print) won't find it so easy. Located as it is above a Starbucks in a site that continually busts businesses and with an entrance off a back alley, those Mojo people must be confident. There are two bars - the one downstairs could be part of any chain, but the dinky upstairs space with great views of, er, Salford is the red beating heart of the Mancunian adventure. But even in the downstairs space, you'll be able to enjoy a music policy of bouncing guitar classics without a trace of insipid house or trance. And ballsy cocktails and beers, such as the superior Chilean offering Cusquena, help build the mood. There's food available from lunch to early evening, with Brit faves and Caribbean classics

House special: Dark and Stormy (Gosling Black Seal rum from Bermuda with Jamaican ginger beer)

Odd

Thomas Street, City

0161 833 0070 8B

Mon-Sat 11am-11pm; Sun 11am-10.30pm

The full-length windows coupled with an interior design scheme that somehow at once suggests both a French colonial café and an NYC Soho bar pull the punters right in. Vibrant red and yellow walls, hookah pipes by the bar and a general air of good-natured naughtiness prevail. Upstairs is a Moroccan snug, whilst downstairs lurks the tiny and intimate basement room where movie projections take place. Regardless of what the name suggests, there's a studied air of class about the place, hinting at the fact that the management know exactly what they are trying to achieve. Odd is a complete bar, ideal for a lunchtime nibble, a mid-afternoon coffee or for a rollicking good night out.

Entertainment: twice monthly film showings, acoustic nights, Sunday chill-out night, DJs at other times
House specials: various beers from around the globe, flavoured gins
Children: welcome before 7pm

Panacea

John Dalton Street, City

0161 833 3000 5D

www.panaceamanchester.co.uk

Mon-Wed noon-midnight; Thu-Sat noon-2am; Sun noon-12.30am

This is one smart place. Designer Bernard Carroll has come up with an interior that performs the clever juggling act of looking comfortable but opulent during the day and glamorous yet suave during the evening. The feature nobody will ever forget is the six metre or so honey-coloured onyx bar. This exudes an air of luxury matched by the prices. The cocktails are excellent - indulge in a Strawberries and cream concoction of vodka, strawberries, coconut and copious amounts of champagne and you'll be more than satisfied. Make sure you dabble in a classic Martini too. Panacea is definitely not a Northern Quarter style place though - this is a dress-up, show-off bar, especially at the weekends. How many blond girls in tight dresses (and older Cheshire ladies who should know better) can there be in the world? The mid-priced meals, miniature but adorable versions of classic bar food such as burgers and so on, are a worthy addition though.

Cocktails: 32 (8 long, 8 short, 8 martini, 8 flutes)
House special: Panacea cosmopolitan
Entertainment: DJs on week nights
Disabled access: full

Rodeo

High Street, City

0161 832 4529 8B

Mon-Sat 7pm-11pm

Rodeo opens its saloon doors to a pick'n'mix of glitzy girls, work-shirted lads and older couples. The tiny venue's interior is red

Rodeo

and western-themed. Drinks are available both from the bar and via waitress table service. Like its neighbour, Socio Rehab, the cocktails are exceptional and the spirit collection is classic and classy. The margaritas are the focus (is this Manchester's first margarita bar?), though, and come properly salt-rimmed with fresh lime or in any number of more exotic combinations.

House special: margaritas

Sola

Contact Theatre, Oxford Road, University

0161 274 0606

Mon-Thu 11am-11pm; Fri-Sat 11am-2pm

Inside the futuristic fortress that is the Contact Theatre, the bold orange and blue colour scheme of Sola provides a suitably lively backdrop for the creative juices to flow. A buzzy pre-performance atmosphere prevails here, probably fuelled by the varied cocktail menu. Sola Bull and the Contact Tea Party are a notable pair, the latter consisting of a potent mix of vodka, rum, gin and tequila. Until 6pm each day, the cocktails are offered at happy hour prices of £3, surely setting

Hotel bars

As anyone who's seen *Lost In Translation* knows, there's just something about a hotel bar. Not every hotel bar, admittedly - you're hardly going to look back fondly at those stolen moments you grabbed at the Premier Lodge at Scotch Corner.

But when all the elements collide just so - the slightly displaced atmosphere of a place *in* the city yet somehow not *of* it, the transient crowd, the whispers and assignations - there really is no better, more rewarding place to spend a few hours as a stranger in your home town.

So which does *City Life* think are the best four in Manchester? The first two provide the best celeb spotting opportunities. Opus at the **Radisson Edwardian** (0161 839 9929 5E) provides opulent, high drama with a splash of red neon. It's very expensive but has a superb glass-protected drinking area in the old arcade of the Free Trade Hall.

The River Bar and Terrace at the **Lowry** (0161 827 4000 4C) is similarly pricey and this time has an external, first-floor terrace over the River Irwell. The River Bar serves the best food - from Eyck Zimmer's exceptional menu.

Less expensive but more spectacular than either of the first two is Tempus at the **Palace Hotel** (0161 288 1111 7G). This takes us back 100 years with a spankingly impressive bar housed in the huge and hansome faienced (glazed tilework) dream hall of the former Refuge Assurance - just look at those arches.

The **Midland Hotel** (0161 236 3333 5E) is a shade younger than the Palace, but was a purpose-built hotel from the start. We're going to cheat here, as the best place to take a drink is not in the bar but in the glorious raised area opposite reception. This resonates with a century of hotel atmosphere. Anybody who was anybody in Britain and beyond stayed here up until very recently, and a thousand Manc men have gone down on bended knee here after a meal at the French with their ladies. In tribute to all those ghosts of past guests, and for its soaring glass-lit ceiling, the Midland (pictured below) gets our vote as best hotel bar.

Bars

New Bars

Uluru

the scene for dramas to be acted out off stage as well as on.

Entertainment: various nights and events - call for info

Children: welcome

Disabled access: full

Uluru

Barlow Moor Road, Chorlton

0161 881 6789

Mon-Wed 11am-11pm; Thu-Sat 10am-midnight; Sun 10am-10.30pm

To find a new Aussie bar amidst the downbeat boho charm of Barlow Moor Road is slightly perturbing. It's decorated in burnt orange (it couldn't have come in any other colour really), but subtlety is key and the emphasis is on style and relaxation. The obligatory leather jacket and Converse wearing crew make their presence known, but so do the more sedate, young professionals. With a surfboard tucked in one corner and some Aboriginal masks and indigenous art on the walls, there are concessions to the land down under in aesthetic terms. Naturally, Fosters is on tap, but there's also usual suspects San Miguel and John Smiths. An interesting addition to the crop of café bars in the area.

House special: Oz wine, unsurprisingly called Uluru

Disabled access: full

The Bar

531/533 Wilbraham Road, Chorlton

0161 861 7576

Mon-Sat noon-11pm; Sun 11am-10.30pm

If you wanted a model cross-generational bar, this is definitely a contender for Manchester's finest. The décor is relaxed but stylish with a nice mixture of substantial tables, converted pews and big leather sofas. The food is even better, putting many a restaurant to shame. The new chef has re-jigged the menu a little, but highlights include seafood linguine crammed with mussels, monkfish, scallops and tiger prawns and their vast veggie breakfast. Now a separate business with Knott Bar from the Marble Arch pub and the nearby Marble Beer House, they still provide the lovely micro-brewery ales from the latter company, such as the lovely ales Manchester Bitter and the distinctive Ginger Marble.

Entertainment: jukebox, Monday night quiz

House special: Manchester Bitter from the Marble Brewery beers

Children: welcome until 6 pm

Disabled access: full

Bar Fringe

8 Swan Street, City

0161 835 3815 9B

Mon-Sat noon-11pm; Sun noon-10.30pm

An old favourite and a pioneer of the idea of the Northern Quarter being the place where independent businesses come to live. This beer drinker's paradise has a rugged and lived-in interior with scattered seating, cartoon and poster festooned walls and bare floorboards. There's an outdoor area too. Despite the fabulous collection of British beers, you can tell that the management have an affection for the small country that has a false

reputation for having no famous people at all: Belgium. The CAMRA guide calls this a Belgian 'Brown Bar', which might be pushing it, but you know what they mean. There's simple food until 6pm, but remember that some of the drinks can double as a nourishing meal. It's a great place to get comfortable and see the evening out with kick-ass flavours courtesy of barley, hops, yeast and water.

Entertainment: Ted, the opera singer

House specials: 15 draught beers (11 keg, 4 cask), 1 traditional cider, foreign ales, Belgian and German beers (plus guest ales and continental beers), 4 pint jug of Hoegaarden for £8.50 on Sundays

Big Hands

Oxford Road, University

0161 272 7779

Mon-Sat noon-2am; Sun 6pm-midnight

Big hands on the outside, warm heart on the inside. Nestled in enveloping couches, musicians, DJs and students slug bottles of beers from far-flung places whilst The Velvet Underground and The White Stripes blare from the jukebox. The central nervous system is the glowing red area of chairs and tables at the rear of the venue, which belies its box-like appearance. The informal atmosphere and regular DJs enhance the experience - well, they usually do. Now an undeniable part of Mancunian life, this University located establishment displays its credentials best by being a bar that attracts people from way beyond the confines of academia.

Entertainment: DJ Monday-Saturday 10pm-2am and Sunday 8pm-midnight, plus live bands and the occasional mini music festival

House specials: there's a full range of continental beers or try the Martini coffee, invented by the owner

Blue Cat Café

17 Shaw Road, Heaton Moor

0161 432 2117

www.bluecatmusic.co.uk

Daily 7pm-1pm

Hey groovy cats, if you live in the southern hinterlands then this is the feline for you - it's even worth the slow 42a bus from town or the direct train to Heaton Chapel station from Piccadilly and the ten-minute walk. The justification for the detour to this pleasantly fitted out indie rogue would be the range of live performance on offer. You get poetry readings, open mic sessions but above all, music and more music. The place even has its own record label - how cool is that?

Entertainment: open mic night Mondays, comedy every third Thursday of the month, live music every night

House special: range of German and Belgian beers

Bluu

Smithfield Market, Thomas Street, City centre

0161 839 7195 8B

www.bluu.co.uk

Fri-Sat noon-2am; Sun-Tue noon-midnight; Wed-Thu noon-1am

Winner of the *City Life* Manchester Food and Drink Festival Bar of the Year 2005 for providing consistent buzz and excitement in this handsome corner of the Northern Quarter. Bluu is a smooth operator that appeals to a broad audience: leftfield clientele from the Northern Quarter, city centre workers and even Deansgate Locks escapees looking for a different view and atmosphere. Or maybe they're all going for the classic and original cocktail mixes - although Socio Rehab across the road would say they do that sort of stuff better. The no-nonsense décor is injected with a splash of the '70s, especially in the

Bluu

sinister and darkly alluring basement. The restaurant area has an intimate yet stylish vibe and the good Modern British food is more than worth tucking into. This being Manchester, and this being an establishment that is part of chain with representatives in Nottingham, Liverpool and so forth, it's elevation to Bar of the Year has been a controversial choice. Still, you can't satisfy everybody, although a visit to the place might assuage most fears as to its suitability for the award.

Entertainment: DJs Thursday-Saturday

House special: Bluumopoliton (Wyborowa peach vodka shaken with peach liqeur, Cointreau, lime and cranberry juice)

Disabled access: full

Centro

72-74 Tib Street, City

0161 832 1325 9B

www.centrobar.co.uk

Mon-Wed noon-11pm; Fri-Sat noon-1pm; Sun noon-12.30am

Part of the discriminating little empire of Cord, Centro and the Rampant Lion, this is a bohemian hotspot, that attracts an edgy (in style and fashion rather than mood) crowd who adore the mix of proper pints from superior local micro-breweries such

as Phoenix plus decent wines and continental beers. The food is best when simple and direct, such as Irish stew with soda bread and butter and Mushroom, lemon and Parmesan risotto. The bargain Sunday breakfasts and roasts are also recommended. Equally simple and functional is the décor both upstairs and downstairs, which borders on the drab - not that people seem to mind.

Entertainment: DJs Friday-Sunday

House specials: Local micro ales and Belgian beers

Children: welcome downstairs until 7.30pm

Comedy Store

Arches 3&4, Deansgate Locks, City

0161 839 9595 4G

www.thecomedystore.co.uk

The clown of the Locks is actually seriously worth a visit. The most famous brand in British comedy set up shop here in September 2000, luring punters into its dark and spacious surrounds. Though the emphasis may rest on the goings-on in the 500-seater auditorium, the decent food and wine list fuel the chuckling. The offer of a combined two-course dinner in the canal-side gallery and tickets for the show make for a superb night out, simple as that.

Entertainment: various comedic acts including plays, stand-up and performance

Disabled access: full

Corbieres

2 Half Moon Street (off St Ann's Street), City

0161 834 338 5C

Mon-Sat 11am-11pm; Sun noon-10.30pm

Tucked away on a side street and down a pokey flight of stairs, the warren that is Corbieres could seem like a safe haven from the bustle of the city centre, but be careful: like many before you, you may be seduced into staying late, drinking deep and ending up like the dimly lit interior - unevenly plastered. In fact, the place shouldn't work at all when you factor in the uncomfortable seating, the run-of-the-mill drinks and the undistinguished menu. Yet somehow Corbieres succeeds. Maybe this is down to the friendly staff or the relaxed atmosphere. It might even stem from the famous jukebox which, with its combination of rock classics and Manc indie faves, has gained an implausibly good reputation.

House specials: traditional beers, wines and spirits

Cord

8 Dorsey Street, City

0161 832 9494 9C

www.cordbar.com

Mon-Sat noon-11pm; Sun 4pm-10.30pm

Small but perfectly formed, Cord is all grown up for its size. It's an important place too - in many ways, this was the model for much of the indie activity going on presently in the Manchester bar scene whether hereabouts or in Chorlton. If you're peckish, get stuck into a hearty pie with side orders

of mash, peas or gravy, washed down by the ever-changing range of continental beers and ales. The crowd is usually made up of musos and students idling in corduroy-clad booths. Various names on the Manc scene inflict their irreverent musical mix on the bar during the weekend, showing that Cord knows how to not take itself too seriously. Pop trivia folk might be interested to hear that the toilets come from the Haçienda - crap fact, but at least we're not taking the piss.

House specials: a selection of export German beers such as Sruh and Bitburger, cherry beers, raspberry beers and a Brit guest ale

Entertainment: DJs Thursday-Saturday 8pm-11pm

Disabled access: partial

Cornerhouse

70 Oxford Street, City

0161 200 1508 8F

www.cornerhouse.org

Mon-Sat 9.30am-11pm; Sun 11.30am-10.30pm

A split-level, split-personality venue. The upstairs cafe sports views of one of Manchester's busiest crossroads, and offers a haven from the hectic. There are good value food ranges from Britain to the Mediterranean with the odd nod to the Orient. Clientele ranges from leftfield intellectuals, artists and cultural commentators to, er, not much else - it's interesting and very Manchester. 'The Reel Deal' on a Monday evening entitles you to a cinema ticket (hence the name), a pizza and a glass of house wine or a pint of Amstel for £10. The downstairs bar is more exciting all round, with consistently challenging and interesting artwork plus good beers and wine. Presently run by the people behind Grinch and Felicinis, the Cornerhouse catering is two decades old in 2005 - just like the arts centre itself.

Cornerhouse

Entertainment: Monday quiz 8.30pm in the bar, DJs Thursday-Saturday in the upstairs bar

Cocktails: to order, happy hour 9pm-10pm £2.95, 5pm-7pm, £9 for a bottle of house wine

House special: Continental beers

Children: welcome until 8pm

Disabled access: full

Fab Café

111 Portland Street, City

0161 236 2019 8E

Mon-Thu 4.45pm-2am; Fri noon-2am; Sat 3pm-2am; Sun 6pm-10.30pm

An acquired taste, but style isn't everything in bar land. Fab is quirky central for Manchester, establishing that eccentricity can be a successful trait. The punters are an eclectic bunch of good timers who make visitors very comfortable. The evening entertainment at this sci-fi themed bar (expect Daleks, Thunderbird models and Space Invaders) is equally varied, but general Mancunian rock and pop mayhem is deployed here most nights of the week. The Fab crowd is varied in age and aspiration too, from students to chief executives (well probably), and all of them want to dance like their lives depend upon it until the lights dim.

The Castlefield Basin

Map: 1,2,3/F,G

A walk around Castlefield is always impressive. Stray off Liverpool Road and you find a strong boned landscape of strutting railway viaducts and a canal basin with an outdoor arena, modern buildings and a part reconstructed Roman fort thrown in. This is a fine place for food and drink, especially in summer in the sun-trapping, car-free terraces of the various food and drink places around here.

Dukes 92 with its new Albert's Shed restaurant (see pgs 125 and 25 respectively) and **Choice** (see pg 32) can be magical. In the actual Basin area, the latter two are the only places worth coming back to on winter days. Remember also the excellent **White Lion** (pg 125) and the **Ox** (pg 131) pubs on Liverpool Road. The other bar in the basin, **Barça** (Catalan Square, 0161 839 7099), has always had an ill-conceived internal design. It's best to get out of the place to either the external, canal-side drinking area or the fine first floor balcony.

On the fringes, **Knott Bar** (see pg 110) is a cracker, and across the road lies **Atlas**, (0161 834 2124) with its fabulous back terrace.

Entertainment: DJs every night from 10pm, Dawn Acton (ex Corrie actor) on Sat/Mon

Children: welcome until 7.30pm

Fat Cat Café

Deansgate Locks, City

0161 839 8243 4G

www.fatcat.to

Mon-Tue 11am-midnight; Wed-Thu 10am-1pm; Fri 10am-1am; Sat 10am-2am; Sun 11am-11pm

This cat got the cream by not following the trend set by the other beasts on the Deansgate Locks strip - Comedy Store excepted. Many people end up in places like the grotesque Loaf not realising that this more discerning venue is just a couple of doors down. With sharper looks from a recentish refurbishment - of course still tied to that great brick vault of the former railway arches - this is a smooth place to grab a meal or try the various drinks, including the broad range of cocktails. The place is on two levels with the basement club right up against Rochdale Canal - ooh the glamour! Fat Cat is a sister venue of Bluu bar (see pg 106).

Entertainment: basement club 'Pussy Boutique' with funky house Friday 9pm-1am, Saturday 9pm-2am

Cocktails: extensive cocktail list and extensive back bar with premium spirits

Children: welcome until 6pm

Disabled access: full

Fuel Café Bar

448 Wilmslow Road, Withington

0161 448 9702

Daily 9am-12.30am

Keeping it simple in the southern reaches of the city, Fuel is a popular veggie venue in the centre of Withington. Proving that vegetarians require ample and filling portions too, the cafe serves substantial portions

Hillary Step

for only a few pounds. There are cooked veggie breakfasts that aren't just presented in the usual plated version but inventively and deliciously wrapped in flour tortillas as fajitas and burritos too. There are also pittas, burritos and hefty salads. All can be washed down with a Lavazza coffee, a herbal tea or something stronger from the licensed bar. Though oddly, the milk used is always skimmed, so sometimes the lattes can seem a little weedy. A recent paint job combines clean cream with a warm, womb-like deep red and a couple of friendly yucca plants add greenery. Daily newspapers are always on hand, while the staff are helpful and friendly. Fuel transforms into a cracking venue for those night-time activities too.

Entertainment: frequent events are staged in the upstairs room

House special: the breakfast fajita

Disabled access: partial

Hillary Step

199 Upper Chorlton Road, Whalley Range

0161 881 1978

Mon-Thu 4pm-11pm; Fri-Sat noon-11pm; Sun noon-10.30pm

The original string of negatives that attended the opening of the Hillary has softened. The 'no smoking, no

sand*bar*

Huge selection of European Beers, draught and bottled Real Ales, Good Pub grub weekdays from 12-2pm and 6-8pm

Enjoy £2 a pint Amstel, scrumptious curry and tunes played by our resident DJ every Wednesday from 8pm. | Join us for chilled out Saturday Sessions with soothing music and £2 a pint Amstel from 2-6pm | All events and room hire free

Knott Bar

music, no vending machines, no food' policy has relaxed with the provision of bar snacks, nibbles and canned but decent music. The opening of the front outdoor terrace in summer has also reaped rewards, finally establishing the Hillary Step as a great community bar in an area that has traditionally been a wasteland for anybody who didn't have the morals of old-style Methodists. The bar design is low key but easy on the eye, with two feature walls of burnished plaster and wax in ruby red and mustard. Look out for the ales, beers and the 13 malt whiskies, including those delectable beauties Laguvulin and Dalwhinnie. It's a shame that un-neighbourly folk have prevented use of the smart looking rear drinking area though - some of that old style Whalley Range puritanism still survives.

Entertainment: jazz night every Sunday from 9pm, quiz night first Tuesday of every month
House specials: Thwaites and guest ales, a selection of continental bottled beers, as well as fruit beers, white beers, and cider
Disabled access: partial

Iguana Bar

115-117 Manchester Road, Chorlton
0161 881 9338
www.iguanabar.co.uk
Mon-Thu & Sun noon-midnight; Fri-Sat noon -12.30am

It's a strange beast, this particular Iguana, a progressive reptile if ever there was one. A hybrid of a '50s diner and a bohemian take-away, it's more of a chameleon than its name suggests - capable of being a comedy venue, a live music haunt and a colourful drinking den seemingly in the blink of an eye. Possessing a range of drinks that would shame much larger establishments, it's apt that its menus are tailored to sating the Chorlton masses and soaking up those boozy vibes. Olives, paninis, chips and dips, chicken naan and falafel, hummus and pitta are the sort of dishes served. Seemingly Iguana can turn its little scampering feet to anything.

Entertainment: Mirth on Monday, Tuesday open mic night, Thursday acoustic gig night, Wednesday bands, Sunday world music night (everything from country to Turkish)
House special: large range of vodkas and world beers, plus good wine list
Children: until 8pm

Jam Street Café

209 Upper Chorlton Road, Whalley Range
Mon-Fri 10am-11pm; Sun 10am-11pm

This back to basics bar has a big following despite its small interior and

is in the area called North Chorlton by estate agents but Whalley Range to the locals. Drinks include standards such as Staropramen and Hoegaarden but there's more variety with the bottled beers and the wines are good too. Food is a top notch for the price with a daily changing choice of two mains, one veggie and one meat or fish. Food is supplied until it runs out or 9pm whichever comes first. The addition in 2005 of an outside terrace, together with that of the Hillary Step, see above, is giving this previously quiet part of the city a more cultivated aspect in summer.

Entertainment: quiz and curry night Wednesdays, DJs Thursdays and Saturdays
House special: Paternina Rioja
Children: welcome

Knott Bar

Deansgate, City
0161 839 9229 3G
Sun-Wed noon-11pm; Thu noon-midnight; Fri-Sat noon-1pm

A wonderful bar in which to relax and let the world fly by - just like its sibling, the Bar in Chorlton (see pg 105). Knott has a laid-back atmosphere, comfy leather chairs and well-stocked but unobtrusive jukebox. The clientele are from a mixed age group looking for a place to chat with fine drinks to boot. In the winter, the décor creates something of a winter retreat, whilst the first floor balcony is ideal for sunny days - shame that it's north facing but at least you can watch the trams pulling in and out of the city. The bar is well-known for its micro brewery selection of organic ales along with fruity and not-so-fruity continental beers and a couple of other interesting guests. It is also one of the best places in which to enjoy draughts and chess. Pubs trying to be bars rarely pull it off. But bars trying to be pubs have a much better hit rate. Knott Bar takes the latter route with notable success.

Entertainment: fabulous jukebox, chess and draughts

Children: welcome

Disabled access: full

Kro Bar

325 Oxford Road, University

0161 274 3100

www.kro.co.uk

Mon-Fri 8.30am-11pm; Sat 10.30am-11pm; Sun 10.30am-10.30pm

The first of the Kro-labelled luminaries to spring up is handily situated for a pre-gig tipple opposite the Manchester University Students' Union. It is a very tasteful venue, part of a well thought through and inspired operation. Chunky furnishings, high ceilings and big windows give a bright and airy feel. The minimalistic downstairs areas contrast nicely with the more homely space upstairs, where you'll find comfy leather couches and artwork on the walls. Heated outside areas front and back and a barbecue in the former keep things interesting through summer. There is a huge selection of imported beers and the food is reasonably priced and tasty. A Kro signature dish is Biksmad, a Danish dish of diced topside of roast beef, potato and onion sautéed in butter, topped with a fried egg and served with beetroot.

Kro 2

Cocktails: to order

House specials: many varieties of lager and real ale, 30 different continental beers, extensive wine list, Danish food

Entertainment: Monday night quiz, DJs on Thursday-Saturday

Kro 2

Oxford Road, next to BBC, City

0161 236 1048

www.kro.co.uk

Mon-Thu 8.30am-midnight; Fri 8.30am-2am; Sat 10.30am-2am; Sun 10.30am-midnight

Kro's younger and much larger sibling, and *City Life* Bar of the Year 2002, is a justifiably popular haunt for Manc workers and students. Occupying the unlikely venue of the former National Computing Centre, Kro 2 has a sharp modern interior the only downside of which is the echo chamber effect of hundreds of happy punters chatting away - the music doesn't help and could do with being turned down occasionally. The grub here puts some of the city's restaurants to shame. Meanwhile, the tree-shaded outdoor terrace under umbrellas and with heaters is the best place to sit down and drink in the city, with the buses ganging up on Oxford Road and the Mancunian Way soaring above - it adds up to a perverse kind of magic. The Kro group also run Café Muse in Manchester Museum (their only dodgy venue) and the excellent Old Abbey pub in Manchester Science Park. A new and huge addition to the Kro family is expected at Piccadilly in late 2005.

Entertainment: DJs from Fat City records on Fridays and Saturdays

House specials: Danish foods (such as Madister plotz - Danish sausage with red cabbage), Peroni on draught and Mexican ale Negra Modelo

Children: welcome if dining

Disabled access: full

Deansgate Locks

Map: 4G

Six bars plus the Comedy Store occupy striding railway arches across a boardwalk over the Rochdale Canal. Here there's a curious coming together of the Cheshire set, lads and lasses from Lancashire towns and a sprinkling of studenty types and tourists. Generally the age group is mixed, but as the night wears on and the volumes are cranked up, the 20s and early 30-somethings take over. A good time to visit is early evening in good weather when it's pleasant on the boardwalk.

All the bars stay open late, most serve food, all have DJs or other entertainment. The biggest venue, and the overbearingly self-important one, is **Loaf**, characterised by decent food, cocktails, big spaces and comfy chairs. At the other end of the row you'll find **Sugar Lounge** (0161 834 1600), the smallest venue with a slightly sinister feel and the most exclusive tag if you like poseurs with bags of money but not necessarily wit. Sugar Lounge is where TV personality Angus Deayton was infamously snared by a young lady. In between is the most individual bar, the **Fat Cat Café** (see pg 108), which has the most urbane crowd. **Arch 9** and **Revolution** could be on any High Street. **Baa Bar** has an interesting range of let's-get-drunk-really-quickly shooters and a galaxy of disco balls.

Lead Station

Lead Station

99 Beech Road, Chorlton

0161 881 5559

Mon-Fri 10am-11pm; Sat-Sun 11am-11pm

A solidly new bourgeois venue in south Manchester's most solidly new bourgeois, New Labour (and Old Labour) suburb. Outside tables and chairs are strewn around, while inside there's an old bit that makes up the bar and a newer bit tacked on which is the dining area. Décor is sort of amateur Lawrence Llewellyn-Bowen without the confidence in vivid colour. The food is okay, with seabass and steak dishes, a couple of veggie things and a very good burger. The Sunday breakfast is the best thing they do. During the afternoons, it can resemble a crèche - with booze for mums and dads eager for a little relaxation time. And now an apology: occasionally *City Life* gets letters because of the persistence in these guidebooks for referring to the place by its nickname of the 'Les Station'. Les Dawson never came here, by the way - we call it that because of its popularity amongst lesbians. Still, the place must be doing something right because it is almost always busy.

Cocktails: to order

House special: the excellent wine list

Children: welcome

The Gay Village Map: 8F

Whether on a brief visit to the city or a longer stay, everybody should stray into this lively neighbourhood. If it all looks a bit familiar too, the chances are that you've seen the area countless times on TV - from the award-winning international hit of *Queer as Folk* to many other Red Production, BBC etc dramas.

Taurus, Velvet and Via Fossa are highlighted elsewhere in this section. Otherwise, stand-out stars include the evergreen (well, ever-ready at least) **New Union**, a cabaret pub and real laugh with late licence and extraordinary drag competitions, **Spirit**, modern and more ooh-la-la with a good roof terrace, the **Rembrandt**, a pub and hotel with a thing for leather, and the **Churchill**, a recently expanded all-singing, all-dancing gayathon. In adjacent streets, you'll find a kitsch **Baa Bar**, a daft but amusing **New York, New York** - check the neon outside - and a dafter **Hollywood Show Bar**. Back on Canal Street, one of the great Manchester bars of the early '90s, **Manto**, has re-opened under its original name, but has yet to re-scale the heights of its former glory. Further down again, past the **Churchill**, is the popular **Queer** from the school of Nigel Martin-Smith, ex Take That manager and Essential club owner. **Vanilla** is a lesbian and gay friends only space. On the way, you will pass the latest addition to the scene, **View**, for good-time, up-for-it girls and boys who enjoy a drink and a laugh.

For info on all the many clubs - **Cruz 101**, **Essential**, **Legends** and diverse others - you'll just have to dig into your pockets and purchase the weekly *City Life* magazine.

Peter Street

Map: 4E

The earthiest of Manchester's party places and the spiritual home of binge drinking. If you go out here, it's best to leave your pretensions behind.

Expect young girls and more mature ladies all dressed in micro-minis and décolletage tops, and lads and older men who think ten pints of Stella is a good aperitif. **Brannigans** advertises itself as the purveyor of 'drinking, dancing and cavorting', which is so true. There's live cabaret and music. Opposite is **Bar 38** with the fabulous grassed theatre and fountains in front, the zany shape and nothing else going for it apart from size. **Life Café**, meanwhile, back over the road, is in much better taste. Putting on frequent decent live music, comedy and other events, the space is strong as well and includes a 200-seater balcony restaurant, a VIP bar and a basement club.

Teasers lies in the corner of the nearby Great Northern Square and displays bargirls and barboys dressed in tight, tiny costumes. Down Quay Street are the **Walkabout** and **Sports Café**. Both are dominated by sports screens, the latter a warning that any bar with the word 'sports' in the title should be avoided. Back at the top end of Peter Street is the anonymous **Baby Grand** and the more recent bar called **Bedlam** - says it all really.

Surveying all of this is the **Radisson Edwardian Hotel**. You can watch the wildlife late into the night from the glassed-in arcade of the old Free Trade Hall here. Very entertaining it is too.

Lime

Lowry Outlet Mall, Salford Quays

0161 869 0440

Mon-Sat 11am-1pm; Sun 11am-12.30pm

Lime isn't the most rock and roll of venues - more the kind of joint that anyone can drop into. Like neighbouring Café Rouge, it's a big space built into the Lowry Outlet Mall, but still has views of the Lowry footbridge that dominates the Quays and overlooks the stunning Lowry arts centre. It's also blessed with a significant outdoor patio for an al fresco tipple. The interior is mixed up: chunks of '70s kitsch wood laminate fight with lime light panels, tiny TV screens and hazardous-looking copper sheeting. The cosy booths around the back wall are a nice touch and overall, it's a spacious and comfortable satellite of the city centre enterprise - and the best place for a drink on the Quays by a mile.

Entertainment: DJ on Saturdays playing classic pop tunes
House special: Flirtini
Cocktails: broad menu of over 45
Children: welcome, but not too late, and separate food menu available
Disabled access: full

Living Room

80 Deansgate, City

0161 832 0083 5C

www.livingroom.co.uk

Mon-Wed 10am-midnight; Thu 10am-1am; Fri-Sat 10am-2am; Sun 11am-midnight

An extraordinarily popular and lively venue that in the afternoon is frequented by office workers with hefty wage packets and in the evening by other Greater Mancunians with similarly well-rounded wallets. The cocktails are exceptional here, with real pride being given to their production. The food is good with frequent menu changes and favours the Modern British approach of gutsy ingredients presented with flair - but you'll need to book ahead if you want it. The design is clean, with the white clarity of the ground floor complemented by the handsome dining room on the first floor. There's also a private members' bar, the Study. It is a dress-up and show-off place and perfect for people who like to flaunt it. Still, you can't help wishing that they'd get rid of that silly plasma screen showing grim attenuated models on a catwalk - it's the 21st century, isn't it? You also get easy listening live music and the satisfaction of knowing that you are drinking in the original Living Room in the UK.

Entertainment: live pianist playing jazz, soul and funk, funky house DJ Fridays and Saturdays
House special: Basil grande, but the place is justifiably proud of its 70 plus cocktails
Children: welcome when dining
Disabled access: partial

Marble Beer House

57 Manchester Road, Chorlton

0161 881 9206

www.marblebeers.co.uk

Mon-Sat noon-11pm; Sun noon-10.30pm

A former beer shop turned into a beer drinker's nirvana, but then again it is part of the same company as the outstanding Marble Arch pub and brewery on Rochdale Road (see pg 124). There's seating out front and a bijou interior mainly in wood with a crumpled, comfortable feel. The punters are very Chorlton, as crumpled and comfortable as the decor, big on social conscience and always keen to debate the issues of the day. Whatever you do, don't go in with a *Daily Telegraph* under your arm and say in a loud voice, "Hey Bubba Bush ain't that bad is he?" Snacks come via the Unicorn Grocery and the beers are organic and vegan - see what we mean?

House specials: Marble beers, plus a changing selection of real ciders
Disabled access: partial

Matt and Phred's

64 Tib Street, City

0161 831 7002 9B

www.mattandphreds.com

Mon-Fri 5pm-2am, Sat 2pm-2am

It's sort of impolite if you don't finish up at Matt and Phred's after a night out in the Northern Quarter. But if you get there earlier than midnight, you won't regret it either. This is the only club in the north dedicated to live jazz and plays host to big names and small. There's a decent range of food too, including pizzas and tapas to keep you primed and ready for the acts. Lots of people choose to sit and enjoy the music and many others prefer to loiter around bar area close to the Tib Street entrance, especially if they prefer the conversation to the jazz. There's an interesting wine selection, such as the lively red Vega del Rayo Seleccionada Rioja. But don't worry: you can still get trashed on bottled lagers if you wish.

Entertainment: live jazz music every night from 10pm, Glenfiddich jam session from 4pm Saturdays
Cocktails: 85 on offer

Moon

Jackson's Warehouse, 20 Tariff Street, City

0161 228 2677 10D

www.moon-bar.co.uk

Mon-Thu noon-11pm; Fri-Sat noon-midnight; Sun noon-10.30pm

Moon is shining on the Piccadilly

Matt and Phreds

Basin and it's already pretty full. The terrace to the front is one of the largest in Manchester and the furthest from passing traffic, although the fact that it is unfenced on its canal side is somewhat unnerving - go easy on the drink and be careful of the those manic Canada geese. The interior is a handsome brick space in this early 19th century canal building. The menu is Mediterranean inspired with ciabattas and pizzas. Service is usually friendly, welcoming and helpful.

Entertainment: funk, soul, house DJs Friday-Sunday
House special: happy hour 5pm-7.30pm on selected spirits, alcopops and draft plus bottles of house wine £6
Children: welcome
Disabled access: full

Night & Day

26 Oldham Street, City

0161 236 4597 9C

Mon-Sat 11am-2am

An institution among Manchester musos and winner of *City Life* Bar of the Year 2004, Night & Day provides a small and smoky stage for local talents and international stars alike. Decked out like a Lower East Side dive, with sticky beer mats, glittery fairy lights and tour posters peeling

off lipstick-red walls, it has a well-worn charm borne of years and years of musical plugging. During the day, it is a relaxed place for young and old to tuck into an all-day breakfast, a dish of marinated olives or one of the many Mexican inspired choices. Prices are cheap, and the bar is crammed full of traditional ales and more unusual choices. At night, the place becomes the musical mecca it is renowned for being, even attracting Hollywood celebrity Keanu Reeves earlier this year. When home-grown heroes like I Am Kloot or Elbow return, it becomes a tightly packed sweat-pit for an amiable and eclectic crowd. Night & Day always has an understandable buzz about it as the hotspot for the most exciting international tours and the venue to endorse tomorrow's major artists, before they sell out.

Entertainment: various pinball/quiz machines and music every night
Cocktails: menu above the bar

Pleasure Lounge

489 Wilmslow Road, Withington

0161 434 4300

Daily 10am-midnight

The vaguely exotic façade, not to mention name, is apt given its range

The Printworks

Map: 7B

Formerly the largest city centre print facility in the UK, this will not be to everybody's taste. Arranged around a central gallery with venues opening off, the Printworks not only provides food and drink but, best of all, a superb multi-screen cinema complex, the Filmworks, with IMAX facility. If you upgrade to the Gallery here, you can eat a proper meal and drink alcohol with your movie - an excellent idea.

In the 20-metre-high main area of the gallery, there is a ceiling projection area, a big screen and lots of neon. The most famous chains here, accessed from Withy Grove, are **Hard Rock Café** and **Tiger Tiger**. HRC is just like every other HRC everywhere else, except here they've given due memorabilia attention to Manchester's exceptional pop heritage. **Tiger Tiger** is beast of a venue with several differently themed world bars, a restaurant and a club. **Wagamama** is part of the well-known noodle chain. Southern USA memorabilia and cuisine inspired **Old Orleans** provides decent enough food for filling up before visiting the neighbouring cinema. It's good for kids too. **Henry J Beans** seems tired now, but supplies a broad range of cocktails. **Nandos** does tasty Portugal meets South African food. **Norwegian Blue** is a huge gaff that despite the name, isn't a Scandinavian porn venture but a vodka bar that does food - like the country it can be cold. **Lloyds No 1** is a Wetherspoons outlet for hard drinking at basement prices.

of inexpensive cocktails and hip continental vibe. More than mere pleasure-seekers, the patrons of this stylish bar are bona fide hedonists who come into their own during the infamous and hugely popular open mic nights. Erdinger Weissbrau, Frambozenbier, Corona, Budvar and Leffe are among the bottled beers and there is Boddies, Guinness and Stella on tap. Work by local artists is occasionally displayed on the walls and major sports events are projected onto a sizeable screen. A Thai platter is among the satisfying dishes boasted by a re-invigorated menu, and a good range of coffees and herbal teas is also on offer. The bar is particularly pleasing during the summer, when punters spill out onto the pavement drinking area.

Entertainment: open mic night Mondays, DJs on Fridays and Saturdays, jazz and acoustic on Sundays

House specials: well-stocked back bar including five different types of rum and four different single malt whiskies

Cocktails: extensive list

Children: welcome during the day

Sand Bar

20 Grosvenor Street, University

0161 273 3141

Mon-Fri noon-11pm; Sat 2pm-11pm

When taking one of the fine pints in Sand Bar, it's tempting to ring through for a Manchester Metropolitan University prospectus. With a bar as easy as this on the doorstep, it'd almost be worthwhile going back into education again. Populated by clued-up students and the like, Sand Bar is a luminary in the so-called Southern Quarter. The alcoves of the converted Georgian townhouse in which it is housed plus the convivial crowd fill the place with a homely ambience. There's good, honest bar food such

Sand Bar

as casseroles, steak and ale pie and daily Polish specials, accompanied by a striking array of draught and bottled beers and a soundtrack from the suitably cool jukebox. A drinkers' and slackers' bliss.

Entertainment: Weird Wednesday Wanderings (a DJ-led selection of chilled, funky, funny and downright odd vinyl), Wednesday is also curry night

House special: Amstel lager

Disabled access: partial

Socio Rehab

Corner of High Street and Edge Street, City

08707 573 422 8B

Mon-Sat 6pm-1am

www.sociorehab.co.uk

A proud little bugger this, convinced of the superiority of Socio cocktails - be careful of sneers if you ask for anything tacky like bottled beer. But you can't deny that it's a smooth little number, full of a cool and trendy mystique. For instance, the Socio nameplate is little bigger than a Kraft cheese slice. The boys here clearly want to give the impression that only the discerning can hook into the Socio zeitgeist. This aura of exclusivity is further emphasised by a trendily simple décor set off by a dark, sinister backroom that is one of the sexiest areas in a Manchester bar. The music, after a year or so, remains standard bar stuff - trip-hop and the like - but the cool crowd of discerning and trend-conscious, even trend-setting, Mancs seem to lap up the whole experience - if they can find the place that is.

House special: any of those lovingly prepared cocktails

Solomon Grundy

447-449 Wilmslow Road, Withington

0161 445 6722

Sun–Thu 11am-11pm; Fri-Sat 11am-midnight

Decked out in bold pastels with a red tiled floor and wooden tables, Solomon Grundy has a distinctly boho feel to it. Situated on the main drag in Withington, it's a comfortable haven in which to while away a few hours with a coffee, peruse one of the newspapers they supply or have a few pints with friends. At Solomon's, you can eat throughout the day from a menu that changes on a regular basis. Start with the English breakfast featuring fine pork and leek sausages, lunch on the Roasted Mediterranean vegetable and Mexican cream cheese ciabatta or consume an evening meal of Jamaican jerk coconut chicken with red beans and rice. Be warned that as the breakfasts are popular at the weekend, you often have to wait, and the service, though usually warm, is on occasion indifferent.

Entertainment: occasionally in the room downstairs
House special: the King Solomon breakfast
Disabled access: partial

Taurus

1 Canal Street, City
0161 236 4593 9E
www.taurus-bar.co.uk

Socio Rehab

Mon-Thu noon-11am; Fri-Sat noon-1am; Sun noon-10.30pm

Relaxed, soulful and ambient, Taurus is one of Canal Street's best and was *City Life* Manchester Food and Drink Festival Bar of the Year, 2003. The bar's concept draws heavily on astrology and has inspired Taurus's managers with a number of newer ventures (Moon and Sola - although Moon is now under different management). Customers are drawn to the chilled and unpretentious feel, to which good cocktails, leather sofas, delicate lighting and a gently soulful playlist all contribute. Nestled in the alcoves, the venue displays modern artworks that are changed every month or so. Staff are friendly and helpful and the food menu is varied and reasonably priced. The Salmon linguini is deliciously rich without being sickly and the hot salads are beautiful. Throughout the week, the music is never obtrusive, making it easy to relax and chat. Definitely one of the most civilised places in the Village.

Entertainment: fringe performance venue
Cocktails: all cocktails are £3 from 4pm-7pm
House specials: Strawberry Daiquiri and Cosmopolitan
Disabled access: full

The Temple

Great Bridgewater Street/ Oxford Street junction, City
0161 278 1610 6F
Mon-Thu 4pm-11pm; Fri-Sat noon-11pm; Sun 5pm-10.30pm

One of the most notable small venues in the city centre, the Temple is also one of the most celebrated. From the ugly duckling of gentlemen's urinal, it has metamorphosed into an almost spotless tidgy bar. It is a haven for the city's musicans, artists and quirky types. Indeed, explorers of indie Manchester should make this a priority visit - if for curiosity value alone. A small variety of draught beers complement a daring selection of bottled beers and spirits. Full of gritty bonhomie, this is a comfortable place to spend an evening's intimate local talent spotting. Great jukebox. Food consists of bar snacks.

Entertainment: various DJs, live performances
House special: continental bottled beers

Le Trappiste

40 Greenwood Street, Altrincham
07963 561 335
www.letrappiste.com

Mon-Fri 6pm-11pm; Sat 12.30pm-11pm; Sun 7pm-10.30pm

Perhaps the worst bar to open in 2005 was Odyssey in Altrincham but *City Life*rs found respite in Le Trappiste, one of the best little bars in Greater Manchester. This happy Belgian number is arranged around a hollowed-out centre leading to convivial upper floors. The predominant colours are mellow yellow and the soft orange/red of bare brick. The beers are the real stars, though. If you're unfamiliar with Belgian beers, follow the menu or ask advice from the enthusiastic staff. Be careful you don't lose your shoe - up on high, you'll see a basket with footwear contained therein, which refers to the tradition of your shoe being taken as deposit against harm or theft to the individual and allegedly flavour enhancing glasses given for each beer. Food (7pm-10pm) includes Vlaamse stovery: Flemish beef stew cooked in beer with dumplings and served with crusty bread. It's table service only, and no standing, so make sure you book at weekends. Beer delivery service within the local area for cases of up to 24 bottled beers - see website.

House special: 12 draught beers including De Koninck, Liefman, La Trappe Blonde and over 70 bottled beers

Children: welcome

Tribeca/Bed

50 Sackville Street, City

0161 236 8300 8F

www.tribeca-bar.co.uk

A fun-filled, fun-loving place on the fringe of the Village and for any passing audience that cares to use it. The interior is vivid in purples and reds and the crowd is a mix of locals, office workers and students. Alongside the drinks there is a menu offering grub such as the New York Strip (sirloin

steak topped with parsley, lemon and garlic butter), platters to share and the like. Downstairs is the curiosity of Bed. The name says it all - you literally take your food and drink lying down like the Romans who founded Manchester two millennia ago. Bed apparently stands for 'beverage, entertainment and dining'.

Entertainment: Tuesday karaoke (in Bed), Wednesday unplugged session, Thursday-Sunday DJs
House special: 4pm-7pm house wine for £5 and all cocktails £3
Disabled access: full

Trof

Landcross Road, Fallowfield

0161 224 0467

Mon-Sat 9am-midnight; Sun 9am- 10.30pm

With its proletarian wooden and brick decor, Trof is a favourite with Manchester's bourgeoisie-in-waiting, and you can see why. Firstly there's the food, which is more refined than anything offered by Fallowfield's fast food outlets. On Fridays, there's Wax On, Wax Off and Saturday offers the beats of DJ Rosco, both of which cater for a 'funky, happy, oddball' crowd. When it comes to Sunday morning fry-ups, it reigns supreme, the cafe's expansion highlighting a gap in the local market. Trof sets a studentville benchmark - it's only a matter of time before it has

competitors.

Entertainment: Monday-Wednesday live music, Thursday-Sunday DJs
House special: wine menus on rotation

Velvet

Canal Street, City

0161 236 9003 8F

This could be in the restaurant section or the bars. Whatever, this is one of the classier joints in the Gay Village, with chandeliers, silken furnishings, a sunken fish tank on the stairs and the general air of a sumptuous Parisian bordello. The service is consistently efficient and has been noted by one *City Life* correspondent as 'drop dead gorgeous'. Just as attractive is the menu, which covers all the Modern British bases and makes Velvet a top spot for a classy lunch or a romantic evening meal. There are two areas: the upstairs bar, a splendid and typically exuberant 2005 addition, and the much-loved basement restaurant. Meanwhile, the al fresco seating should ensure that daytime trade doesn't completely pass Velvet by during summer. The metallic flock wallpaper in the disabled loo must make it the most exotic in the land.

Entertainment: DJs Thursday-Sunday
House special: 4pm-7pm house wine for £5 and all cocktails £3
Disabled access: full

Velvet

Via Fossa

Canal Street, City

0161 236 6523 8F

Mon-Thu 11am-1am; Fri-Sat 11am-2am; Sun noon-12.30am

Via Fossa's interior is an impressive jumble of 'medieval' architecture, with wooden staircases, bare brick walls, ornate wrought iron frames and decadent mock candelabras (with light bulbs). In the centre, the open space makes the ceiling appear vaulted, with various levels creating balconies around the basement club. Drinkers can have a bird's eye view of the basement dancefloor, which is excellent for talent spotting. With loud pop music every weekday and plenty of house at the weekends, Via Fossa is a choice venue for strutting, posing and vogueing. People milling around are generally fashionable men with feathered hairstyles, but football shirts and women are not out of place. Tourists may be attracted by Via Fossa's small screen appearances in hit shows *Queer as Folk* and *Bob and Sue*. The food here is also very good. The bar has a separate restaurant with a wide selection of Brit favourites and international dishes that serves until 10pm.

Entertainment: regular theme nights like beach parties, beauty contests and drag entertainment
House specials: 2 cocktails for £5.50 and double vodk & Red Bulls for £2.95 any day of the week
Cocktail: A Girl's Dream is the most popular from an extensive cocktail menu

Waxy O'Connors

Printworks, Withy Grove, City

0161 835 1210 7B

www.waxyconners.co.uk

Mon-Wed noon-11pm; Thu noon-midnight; Fri-Sat noon-1am; Sun noon-10.30pm

Zinc

Does the world needs any more of these Emerald Isle themed nostalgia trips that ruin countless cities in every continent with their baleful presence? Is there an O'Sheas in Ulan Bator? I bet there is. But hold on a second, because Waxy's in Manchester is actually pretty good. First there's the design, which comes in a power blast of timber as though to a design by that perspective-bending artist Escher. In fact, this is the sort of place you can get lost in when returning from the toilets (which could be a plus if your date isn't scintillating company). The added indulgence of sticking a big old dead tree down one side only adds to the enjoyment. The menu is loosely Irish themed but peppered with your regular upmarket pub options like Seafood chowder and Stuffed chicken. Stick with the dozen Rossmore oysters with soda bread to get in the proper swing of things though, and there's a good Irish stew too. Sort of fun, sort of weird, Waxy's is a cut above most other Printworks venues.

Entertainment: diverse promotions including oyster festivals, live music and event
House special: get a Guinness down your neck

Zinc

The Triangle, Hanging Ditch, City

0161 827 4200 6B

www.conran.com

Mon-Thu 10am-midnight; Fri-Sat 10am-2am; Sun noon-10.30pm

This comes from design darling Sir Terence Conran's stable. Thus the smart, cool design is immediately obvious. The venue is split into two levels: food on the mezzanine and soft seating for slouching and slurping in the basement. Zinc is a sassy place full of well-dressed, good-looking types, particularly at the weekends - it's a place to see and be seen. The food (noon to close), with principally, modern European influences, is very good, for instance the Roast halibut, grilled asparagus and shrimp butter. Zinc is especially handy as a pre-shopping warm-up or a post-shopping wind-down.

House special: 30 cocktails including the Flirtini champagne cocktail.
Entertainment: regular DJs, live music, art shows etc
Children: welcome in restaurant but no separate menu
Disabled access: full

Pubs

Pub intro

Humourist Hilaire Belloc decreed in the early 20th century that "once you have lost your pubs, you will have lost the last of England". There's perhaps some truth in this. If a country is defined by qualities that are uniquely its own then pubs are an item that reach to the core of Britishness. Indeed, if a visitor wants to leave behind the tourist sites and hotels for a while and reach under the skin of this nation, a visit to the pub and a chat with the locals is the most accessible and quickest route.

What makes a good pub? Is it an atmosphere of age, beautiful fittings and fixtures? Is it talkative locals and a friendly landlord or landlady? Is it finely kept real ales? It's actually all or a combination of these. The really good pub should tempt you in for a quick half and make you feel so comfortable you stay all night.

The pubs in this section include many such classics, but a fair share of curiosities. Sadly, we couldn't include everything, so the **Beehive** in Glossop (which has a Namibian boxing champion working behind the bar), the **Snipe** in Dukinfield (which has a Harrier fighter plane parked in the beer garden) and the **Royal Oak** in Ramsbottom (which hosts the World Black Pudding Throwing Championship in September) had to be left out.

With the November changes to the licensing laws, opening times have defeated us. Most landlords are playing it by ear until they have found out what's best for their particular pub.

Three city centre crawls

This year we've decided to look at the best city centre pubs by three pub crawls covering the central, the north and the south of the city. All three crawls have separate character and all involve pubs with lots of character, some of them full of right old characters - if you get our drift. There are boozers with celebrity links, good entertainment pubs and some with remarkable interiors or with a fabulous range of ales. All the crawls are approximately 2 kilometres (1.2 miles) long.

Central tour – the heart of the matter

This tour could be called the twin cities tour as it winds its way through the commercial and administrative core of Manchester before crossing the river and ending up in Salford and the area around Chapel Street. The latter part of the tour has even been given an official seal of approval with the Chapel Street Ale Trail from Salford City Council.

Begin at the **Old Grapes** (Little Quay Street, 0161 839 4359 4E), which relocated here from Deansgate a few decades ago. It now sits proudly in Sunlight House, designed by Joe Sunlight in 1932. The latter gentleman loved celebrity, so arranged for Hollywood actor Douglas Fairbanks to come over and open the swimming pool that bears the actor's name and is now part of the Living Well Health Club. The Old Grapes is also in love with celebrity, owned as it is by Liz Dawn who plays Vera in *Coronation Street*. You won't see much of Liz behind the bar but you will see photo shrines to her at each end of the building: Liz with Tony Blair, Liz with the Queen, Liz with the Pope. Bless. The pub serves standard pub grub at lunch, a predictable range of drinks and is popular with office workers and Peter Street party-goers.

Leave the building, turn right onto Quay Street and then left to Deansgate. Cross Deansgate, turn left and take the first right up Bootle Street to the **Sir Ralph Abercromby** (35 Bootle Street, 0161 834 1807 5E), which is 200 years old and was named for an aged but popular British general who died in the Napoleanic Wars in Egypt in 1801. The pub is reputedly haunted by a Peterloo Massacre victim who died on the bar on 16 August 1819. Peterloo began as a meeting demanding representation in Parliament - Manchester had no MP at the time - and was held between today's Midland and Radisson Edwardian (Free Trade Hall) Hotels. Spooks aside, the Abercromby is a pleasant pub that has a cute outside drinking area, good ales such as Timothy Taylor's Landlord and lunchtime food. It maintains the military link every last Saturday of the month with a meeting of gentlemen who adore and trade model soldiers - the toy ones, just in case anybody suspects a double entendre.

Leave the Abercromby and continue up Bootle Street, take a left on Southmill Street and then a left down Jackson's Row to the **Old Nags Head** (19 Jacksons Row, 0161 832 4315 5E). This is the prime pool pub of the city, with four tables in the room upstairs, plus B&B if you need it. There're also lots of events such country music on Sunday evening and karaoke every Friday and Saturday.

Leave the Nags Head by the entrance opposite the way you came in and turn right up Lloyd Street to Albert Square. Turn left and continue over the traffic lights at John Dalton Street onto Cross Street. Turn right up Tib Lane to the **Town Hall Tavern** (20 Tib Lane, 0161 832 3550 6D). The name refers to the original Town Hall, completed in 1825, on King Street - you can see part of the façade re-erected at Heaton Park Boating Lake - not the present structure you've just passed. This is a lovely little pub with good lunchtime food and wines as well as a range of real ales such as Deuchars and Bass. You couldn't pick a more perfect place for a meeting, especially in the upstairs function room - the friendly staff will provide good tucker to accompany the occasion as well. Throughout its history, the Tavern has suffered grievous ignominies - in the '70s it was a topless bar whilst in the '90s it became part of the hideous Flares group.

Retrace your steps down Tib Lane to Cross Street and turn right until you see the handsome terracotta façade of **Mr Thomas's Chop House** (see food pubs, pg 130) on the other side of the road. After a visit, return to the Cross Street and John Dalton Street junction and turn right down the latter street past Joseph Holt's early 1990s pub the **Ape and Apple** (28 John Dalton Street, 0161 236 9645 5D). Stop off for a cheap pint or some gorgeous bottled take-outs such as Thunderholt (4.5%) and Humdinger (3.5%).

Otherwise, continue over the Deansgate junction onto Bridge Street to the **Bridge** pub (see food pubs, pg 130). You could turn right just before the Bridge 10 metres down Southgate to visit the best Irish themed pub in the city centre at **Mulligans** (12 Southgate, 0161 288 0006 4D). Formerly the Waggon and Horses, this is another haunted pub - ask landlord Mr Tremayne Newton if you want some interesting stories. It's also a convivial and jolly pub, with good Guinness and decent pub food.

Carry on down Bridge Street and cross over the River Irwell into Salford. Immediately on your left down by the water is the **Mark Addy** (New Bailey Street, 0161 832 4919 4C), the most recent of the boozers on this trail from the 1980s. Expect guest ales and a famous lunchtime combination of cheeses and patés

as well as other dishes. The pub occupies a converted part of the former landing stage from the days when the Irwell was an important trade and passenger route. The name commemorates local hero, Mark Addy (1838-90), who saved more than 50 people from drowning in the toxic soup that masqueraded as a river. For his efforts, he was awarded the Albert Medal by Queen Victoria. His death was said to have been hastened by swallowing so much filthy water. Fortunately, the Irwell is much cleaner now and one of the big attractions is to sit out on the splendid terrace at the Mark Addy during summer.

The big sandstone blocks that make up the rear of the vaulted main space in the pub not only provided a river frontage but also helped support the New Bailey Prison. This was built in 1790 and stood just above where the Mark Addy sits. Here public executions were held in the 1860s. These were some of the more drunken occasions in the two cities' calendars, with people turning up the day before to get the best

position for the following morning's entertainment - attended, of course, by several beer sellers.

Leave the Mark Addy and return to the street. Turn left down New Bailey Street, under the railway bridge to Chapel Street. A little way up to the left on Chapel Street stood the Moonraker pub. This was made famous in Harold Brighouse's play *Hobson's Choice*, and then later in the novel and the movie of the same name. The latter starred Charles Laughton as Henry Hobson. It was in the Moonraker that Henry sought solace in the bottom of a glass whilst musing on the ingratitude of children and cultivating 'a pleasing vacancy of the mind'.

Continue over Chapel Street to Bloom Street and the wonderful **Kings Arms** (11 Bloom Street, Salford, 0161 832 3605 3B) - the *City Life* Manchester Food and Drink Festival Pub of the Year 2005. This is a classic pub dating from 1874 with progressive attitude. The main room is an adorable oval - you can't get more comfortable than drinking in an egg. The pub has

City Life **Pub of the Year, the Kings Arms**

Detail of the ceiling at the Crown and Kettle

its own in-house theatre company called Studio Salford, and hosts plays and cabaret upstairs every month - see www.studiosalford.com. Wednesday night is jazz night, while other nights are home to live acoustic sessions and the first Tuesday of every month is for comedy. The pub can lay claim to having the best jukebox around. It has simple food - steak and chips, a selection of curries and sandwiches, with a bargain Sunday roast too. Cask ales include four to six changing ales plus Salford's very own and very excellent micros Bazens' and Facer's.

Northern crawl – the wild frontier

Venture into the dark heart of Manchester drinking with plenty of atmospheric if occasionally down-at-heel pubs. If you love Britain's 2,500 plus ales, this is a great place to fast track an induction course into their myriad flavours. The trail includes two of the most splendid interiors in Manchester, with the Crown and Kettle and the Marble Arch, whilst the Hare and Hounds provides more low-key but just as satisfying pub atmosphere.

Start at the **Unicorn** (26 Church Street, 0161 834 8854 8C). This is a handsome, multi-roomed pub with an interior that dates from the 1920s, although the pub has been on this site much longer. The two rooms on the right as you enter from Church Street are particularly good, whilst the magnificent bar is like a ship in full sail. The atmosphere inside is very traditional and very local, a favourite of many of the older folk who used to work in the markets. Manchester Jazz Society meet regularly upstairs.

Leave the pub by the Church Street entrance and turn right to Oldham Street then left up Oldham Street until you reach the **Castle Hotel** (66 Oldham Street, 0161 236 6515 9C). Behind the crazy skewed lettering on the façade, you'll find a bar smack bang in front of you. This is the only tied Robinson's pub in the city centre, often stocking the full range of ales - nine - from the Stockport brewery. The Castle is one of those unchanged survivors - perhaps the nearest the city centre comes to a rural local. Immediately behind the bar is the old snug, now a piano room and behind that down a corridor is the games room with pool, pinball, darts, a jukebox and occasionally live bands. The Castle

has been the adopted home from home for generations of Mancunians and visitors alike. During the 1996 European Championships, the Czech fans adored the place - which explains the flag.

Continue straight up Oldham Road and over Great Ancoats Street to the **Crown and Kettle** (2 Oldham Road 9B) and one of the most astonishing pub interiors around, dating from an undetermined time in the 1840s or 50s. Huge Gothic timber pendants hang down from a ceiling alive with crazy quatrefoil (fourleaf) tracery. The pub was closed for 15 years prior to reopening in October 2005 and suffered arson. The interior shows the distressed but cleaned ceiling in the lounge and how it originally might have looked when painted in the vault. It's a shame that all the rooms have TVs, but at least there are superb ales courtesy of local micros Bank Top, Marble Beers and Boggart Hole Clough as well as Tim Taylor's Landlord. Food is simple, but when the ceiling is this fancy that suffices. The funniest story about this pub reflects its three entrances. In 1950, when a drunk tried to get in but the landlord threw him out, he tried in the next entrance and then the next with the same result. At the third, he asked the landlord, "How many bloody pubs do your run around here".

Leave the pub, locate Swan Street at the western end of the junction here and follow it (you pass Bar Fringe - see pg 105) to the **Smithfield Hotel** (37 Swan Street, 0161 839 4424 9B). This has regular beer festivals, a local in-house ale, the Phoenix Smithfield, pool and B&B if you're feeling exhausted.

Turn left on leaving the pub, walk to the traffic lights then turn right up Rochdale Road. On the left at the junction with Gould Street, you'll find the **Marble Arch** (73 Rochdale Road, 0161 832 5914 www.marblebeers.co.uk 9A), a pub to rival the Crown and Kettle. Built in 1888 for McKenna's Harpurhey Brewery, the Marble, as it became known due to its exuberant design, is now home base to the wonderful Marble Beers. The original interior details of tile and mosaic are spectacular - note the red roses for Lancashire and the tiled frieze of drinks on offer, including gin and whisky. Adjacent to the comfortable back room and visible through a window is the brewing equipment that makes the fine stuff you drink - tours can be booked at the bar. Some of the beers produced here are Marble Bitter, Manchester Bitter, Ginger Marble, Lagonda IPA plus seasonals. The beers are all vegan and all organic. Other guest beers and a cider or perry are stocked at the bar. There's good, wholesome food until 8pm and a jukebox in this fabulous boozer too.

Now backtrack down Rochdale Road a little way until you see the **Beer House** (6 Angel Street, 07868 897075 9A) on your right. This has a well-used (to be kind) interior but provides lots of good ales and has a reputation as a good cider house.

Return to Rochdale Road and turn right. After the lights, the street becomes Shude Hill and just before the tram lines, you'll see on the left hand side another cracking pub, the 200-year-old **Hare and Hounds** (46 Shudehill, 0161 834 9088 8B). This is run by one of the great Manchester landladies, Maxine - a perfect host, friendly and informative, but firm when needed. Outside, the pub has a handsome yet slightly austere green-tiled façade whilst inside it splits into four if you include the function room upstairs. There's a lounge, a basic but comfy vault with TV and darts and a long lobby that doubles as the venue for the traditional Wednesday sing-a-long session - very interesting. Good period detail survives in the tile, wood panelling and etched glass. Food is simple

- snacks, sandwiches, pickled eggs and the like. Beers include Holt's lovely bitter. The folk club, Full Circle, meets upstairs on Friday evenings.

Southern crawl - easy does it

In some respects, this is the most well-mannered of the three tours, starting off in pretty Castlefield and finishing close to the Town Hall. It crosses some grand urban landscapes and includes two very modern pubs as well as three of Manchester's most beloved specimens: the Britons Protection, the Peveril of the Peak and the Circus.

Begin at the well-appointed **Dukes 92** (19-20 Castle Street, Castlefield, 0161 839 8646 www.dukes92.com 2G). Dukes is now as much part of the city drinking scene as the White Lion up the road, and is the best boozer in the Castlefield basin itself. The name arises from the building's former use as stables on the Duke of Bridgewater canal and its location adjacent to the 92nd lock

of the Rochdale Canal. The pub is airy, bright and tasteful. The oldest section still has comfy, classic furniture and an art gallery upstairs. Outside is the best sun-trap drinking area in the city, with a well-used stage. The substantial portions of bread with paté or cheese as well as other meals are renowned. There's a good range of drinks, including cask ales and wine. See also Albert's Shed (pg 25).

Leave Dukes by the bigger of the outdoor drinking areas and walk to the canal bridge, turning right along Duke Street up the hill under the viaducts and past reconstructed Roman bits and bobs up to Liverpool Road. Immediately on the right is the late 18th century building that houses the Ox (see food pubs, pg 131). Turn right up Liverpool Road to the **White Lion** (43 Liverpool Road, 0161 832 7373 3F), which also dates back to the late 18th century. There is a fine range of ales available here and another good outdoor drinking area. Part of this lies in the excavated foundations of the vicus (town) built outside the

The White Lion, Castlefield

Roman fort of Mamucium.

Continue up Rochdale Road to the junction with Deansgate and take a dog-leg across the latter to Great Bridgewater Street under the 157-metre shadow of Beetham Plaza - soon you'll be able to take a drink in the 23rd floor bar of the Hilton Hotel. After trawling under the bridges on the south side of G-Mex, you'll see the **Britons Protection** (50 Great Bridgewater Street, 0161 236 5895 5G) on the other side of Lower Mosley Street.

This is a multi-roomed gem full of elegant wood, tile and plaster detailing 200 years of pub history - it was *City Life* Pub of the Year in 2002. The straight-from-the-street bar area is particularly handsome - note the ceiling. But also try the cosy snug behind and, if sunny and warm, venture into one of the most unsophisticated but oasis-like pub gardens in the city.

Aside from the pints of Jennings, Robinson's, a guest and so forth, you should take a sip or two from the 230 plus whiskies (mostly malt) and bourbons. The first floor function room is a rare survivor but adorned with such tasteless 1970s murals that they've probably become fashionable again. It plays host to a variety of gigs, clubs and associations. Lunchtime food offers good value and good quality, such

as the Tatton Park venison pie and Wild boar and pheasant pie in red wine sauce.

Turn right out of the Britons to **Peveril of the Peak** (127 Great Bridgewater Street, 0161 236 6364 5G) - another gem, albeit in a more unassuming way than its nearby buddy. This late Georgian end terrace has lost its fellow houses but gained (in the 1890s) an emerald external tiling scheme with Art Nouveau lettering. Internally, the design is period but maverick, the weirdness climaxing in the triangular, squashed bar area with the legendary period table football. The Pev was winner of the *City Life* Pub of the Year in 2003 and holds cask ales such as Tim Taylor's Landlord and Wells' Bombardier. Other games include pool, darts and cards, and there is as a well-established Irish folk night on Tuesdays.

Across the road is **Rain** (80 Great Bridgewater Street, 0161 235 6500 www.jwlees.co.uk 5G), a smart modern pub from local brewer JW Lees. This is a popular place, especially at weekends, and has an especially good terrace down to the Rochdale Canal. There's food available plus Lees' excellent ales, including the very strong Moonraker 7%.

Follow Great Bridgewater Street to its junction with Oxford Street (the

old urinal here is now the Temple bar - see pg 117). Turn left on Oxford Street and then right on Portland Street. Cross over Princess Street. Tucked back from Holt's pub the Old Monkey and next to the humorously titled chippy Portland Plaice, you might spot the **Circus Tavern** (86 Portland Street, 0161 236 5818 7E).

This provides proper minimalism - in size rather than aesthetic. How this little beauty survived is a wonder - perhaps it's down to having very few landlords in its 200-year history. The most peculiar feature is a bar so small (perhaps the smallest in the UK) that it fits the bar person and no one else. There's an interesting pub history panel near the entrance and a playing-it-safe back room dedicated to Manchesters United and City. George the landlord is an entertainment himself - once he starts telling his stories, you might never leave. Crisps and snacks are left on the few tables for guests to snack on. If you love pubs, you have to visit this place.

Turn left out of the Circus and take the first left down Nicholas Street past the Chinese Arch. Continue straight over the tram lines onto Booth Street and then first left into Cooper Street. You should be able to see, to the right, the late Georgian **City Arms** (48 Kennedy Street, 0161 236 4610 www.thespiritgroup.com 6E). This is a busy little conversation breeder with one of the best ranges of beer in the Half Square Mile - as Manchester's business district is called. Predictably popular with office workers and with Town Hall staff, the City Arms cuddles and coddles every type of citizen. Cask ales include Tetley bitter and mild, plus six guests, and there's even a guess the mystery ale competition on Fridays. Lunchtime food is available as well.

On one side of the City Arms is the more rough and ready **Vine** (0161 236 3934 6E), and on the other is the rear entrance of the **Waterhouse** (67/71 Princess Street,

Bill Bryson props up the bar at the Peveril of the Peak

0161 200 5380 6E), perhaps the city centre's best representative of the Wetherspoon's chain, providing the usual mix of drink and food only in slightly more upmarket surroundings than usual.

Backstreet pubs

Some of the Northern Crawl pubs could double up as these babies. This little section is included for people for whom an unreconstructed pub down a tiny alleyway or off the main drag has attained a patina of gritty romance, or simply offers an escape into the fug-filled, make-believe land of pure pub. It would be too far to walk between them all unless you're feeling energetic, but try to fit in a visit sometime.

Let's start with the pub furthest from the city centre. This is the **Queen's Arms** (4-6 Honey Street, Red Bank, 0161 834 4239). The Queen's was winner of *City Life* Pub of the Year 2002 and lies in a zany location where warehouses go to die. It also has a quirky clientele of beer monsters, travellers, occasional Vikings (see below) and bemused customers who've read about the place and wondered what on earth they've stumbled upon. No matter - after a couple of drinks, they learn to love the place.

The façade is a handsome tiled affair, this time a shade over 100 years old, behind which lies a couple of comfortable rooms that are full of eclectic bric-a-brac and a real fire. The food is winningly cheap - Sunday and Saturday roasts are £5.50, Chicken Madras is £4 - but the range of beers is the star. At the rear is a huge beer garden with children's play equipment, rabbits, barbecue options and a view of the city centre and the noble CIS tower, there's a good jukebox and cask ales include Timothy Taylor, Phoenix Bantam, plus six guests and Belgian Kriek, St Louis Kriek. There's a quiz every Tuesday (9pm) and darts, pinball and quiz machine.

The Circus Tavern

Club meetings include Triumph motorcycle owners on Tuesdays and the Viking Re-enactment Society on Thursdays.

Not so far away is the **Dutton Hotel** (37 Park Street, 0161 834 4508). This lies close to the old Strangeways brewery of Boddingtons and is a triangular boozer with three rooms all presenting a different face, but filled with bric-a-brac and brasses and so forth. It's owned by Manchester brewery Hydes and is the best escape from a Phil Collins/ Mariah Carey/ WWF wrestling gig in the MEN Arena if by some insanity you wind up with a ticket. There's an outdoor drinking area - it's not brilliant for views though. Cask ales include Hydes bitters and their seasonal range.

Crossing over into Salford and just off Trinity Way is the **Eagle** (19 Collier Street, off Greengate, Salford, 0161 832 4919 4A). If any pub fits the photofit of a backstreet local then it's this place. The inside of the pub is so intimate, you

are bound to get dragged into a conversation with the locals - don't venture in for a quiet drink. The pub is known locally as 'the Lamp Oil' for reasons that remain unclear. Cask ales are the usual quality Holts range, while cards and darts are on offer - Manchester darts, mind. Unlike the national board, a Manchester dartboard has no trebles, a different numbering system and is traditionally called a 'log end', because that is exactly what it is and has to be soaked to be played.

Finally, if your train is delayed at Piccadilly, why not take a walk to the tiny **Jolly Angler** (47 Ducie Street, 0161 236 5307)? This is another Hydes house from the first half of the 19th century - this time with an Emerald Isle flavour. It's been in the same family for a couple of decades and has a real fire and occasional Irish folk music on Sundays. Cask ales include Hydes bitter and seasonal ales. .

Winter ales

The best real ale festival around is the CAMRA Winter Ales Festival, which takes place 19-21 January 2006 at New Century Hall, on Corporation Street, in the city centre.

Bitter sweetness

Manchester is the capital of ale. Check out the Campaign for Real Ale's *Good Beer Guide* and they list 23 independent breweries across the conurbation. Merseyside has 5, the West Midlands has 10 and the whole of mighty London with its teeming millions a mere 10 also. We always knew there was something wrong with that lot.

This doesn't even tell the whole story. Four of Manchester's independents are major multi-million pound concerns: the family businesses of Holt's, Lees, Hydes and Robinson's. The famous Boddingtons bitter is now brewed under licence at Hydes.

Joseph Holt (0161 834 3285) is the brewery nearest to the city centre. Founded in 1849, it brews a very strong and very cheap bitter of 4% strength as well as mild and seasonals. The bitter's the star and despite the occasional poor barrel, is outstanding value - just about the cheapest undiscounted real ale anywhere in the kingdom.

A few miles further north is **JW Lees** (0161 643 2487) brewery. Located at Middleton Junction, Lees was founded in 1828. It brews a full range of beers, bitter and mild, as well as Moonraker, a sock-blow-offer at 7%. A range of seasonal beers are now also produced. The seasonal Harvest Ale is remarkable and gets better with age - it's also 11.5%. It is brewed once a year for release on 1 December and is a limited edition

vintage to celebrate the first brew from each year's harvest of barley and hops.

In Moss Side close to the city centre is **Hydes** brewery (0161 226 1317), founded in 1863, again offering good value bitters and milds with seasonal options that are gaining a national reputation for their excellence.

Seven miles southeast in the suburb town of Stockport is **Robinson's** (0161 612 4061), founded in 1833, with a range of beers including the devilishly potent Old Tom at 8.5%.

Then we have the micros too. All these have their strengths - well, most of them at least. A particular *City Life* favourite is **Phoenix**

Brewery in Heywood (01706 627009), another is **Marble Beers** (0161 819 2694) based at the back of the Marble Arch pub (see pg 124) on Rochdale Road. Other winners include **Bazens'** and **Facer's**, which share premises in Salford (0161 708 0247, 0161 792 7755), and **Bank Top Brewery** in Bolton (01204 595800). Then there's **Mayflower Brewery** (Wigan, 01257 400605), **Leyden** (Bury, 0161 764 6680), **Boggart Hole Clough** (Moston, 0161 277 9666), **Greenfield** (Greenfield, 01457 879789), **McGuiness** (Rochdale, 01706 711476), **Saddleworth** (Uppermill, 01457 820902), **Shaws** (Dukinfield, 0161 330 5471), **Three Rivers** (Stockport, 0161 477 3333) and **Owl** (Oldham, 01706 840356).

Binge drinking – an apology

It came as shock to most Britons in 2003 to hear the Government and the medical profession declare we had become a nation of binge drinkers. We thought we'd been that all the time. It's part of our history. The Romans were the first to notice the alcoholic intake of these islands, complaining about Celtic drinking 2,000 years ago, whilst the Anglo-Saxons were renowned for wassailing the night away. In Manchester in 1608, football was banned largely because of the excessive drinking that took place around the games. From around the same time come the carvings of people 'enjoying' drink on the façade of the Shakespeare pub on Fountain Street in the city.

Ruth Roberts, looking back at her childhood in Edwardian Salford, wrote: '"Beer!" my father would brawl whenever some elder dared chide his tippling. "Beer is my food!" To maintain his strength he seldom drank less than four quarts a day.' And it wasn't only the men - late-19th century Mancunian, Nancy 'Dickie' Bird, was arrested over 170 times as result of drink.

Britain's history is shot through with examples of the misery of drunkenness, but also of how drink has been the lubricant in millions of celebrations - as Lancashire and England cricket maestro Andrew Flintoff showed after the 2005 Ashes victory.

Nor do people need to be told that they drink too much. Part of the diary of Edmund Harrold, peruke-maker (wig maker) survives from 1712 and13:

'17 July 1712 Good business and I sober at eight o'clock at night, but I was merry before I went to bed. 16/9/1713 Fell a drinking all day. 17/9/1713 Drank at several places - the 'Goose', 'Horse and Dog'. 1/8/1713 Am in a miserable condition with drink. 16/8/1713 Dr Ainscough told me plain he would not marry me, because I was a madman in drink and the woman ran her ruin in marrying me [his third time]. By God's help I will observe these rules: 1) Not to drink any strong drink in the morning; 2) Not above a pint at a sitting of business; 3) As little as possible in public-houses. 19/8/1713 Saw Ann, was with her five hours. We concluded to get married in the morning. 20/8/1713 But it's mist; the reason was she could not get time to-day. [Enigmatic entry - maybe she saw sense, maybe she was a servant and could not get time off work]. 23/10/1713 Bless God I've not spent 1d in an ale house for nine days. 3/8/1714 Heard this day of Queen Anne's death. 19-20/9/1714 Finished the Coronation of King George with lying near 2 hours in the dungeon; ill-hurt of face, lost handkerchief, and indeed deserve all for being drunk - it shall be the last time ever. 21/9/1713 As I now think I will leave off drink. 22/9/1713 Am in a miserable condition with drink.'

The present campaign to make the Brits stop bingeing will no doubt fail just as poor Edmund's did. In the end, it's about freedom of choice and the new Puritans can't deny us that. Perversely, the one measure that will ease pressure on people drinking too quickly (if not too deeply), the scrapping of the old restrictions on licensing laws that takes place in November 2005, has been opposed by the new Puritans. Very strange. They just don't want us having our fun, do they? Cheers.

City food pubs

Four pubs stand out in the city centre for the quality of the food they offer. All can, of course, be enjoyed simply as a place to enjoy a drink. But if you want to enjoy food as well, these are a good bet.

The Bridge

Bridge Street, City

0161 834 0242 4D

www.thebridgemanchester.co.uk

This is a fine re-invention of a Manchester pub by Manchester Food and Drink Festival Chef of the Year 2004, Robert Owen-Brown. The Bridge is superb in every way, in décor, in atmosphere and above all in food. Owen-Brown provides an object lesson in what so-called Modern British cooking should really

be about. You'll find a changing menu of lamb, beef and game, plus clever and perfectly cooked fish and seafood dishes - vegetarians are well catered for too. Owen-Brown's take on Spam fritters remains one of the great Manchester retro-food re-enactments, but try a dish such as Braised breast of lamb with bacon, RS Ireland black pudding, rosemary and garlic (£9) and you'll understand the fuss. The wine list is simple but not routine with an interesting range. Upstairs is the sweetest function room just about anywhere - 150 years or so ago this hosted the Manchester Glee Club, whose members loved food, drink, laughter and music and liked to celebrate them big style. Cask ales: Old Speckled Hen and changing guest. Games/ents: themed film nights, gourmet evenings and so forth. Children: welcome. Disabled access: full.

Game at the Bridge

The English Lounge

64 High Street, City

0161 832 4824 5D

A good-looking place with a comfy pub downstairs and a handsome restaurant upstairs. This is notable for a collection of big drapes, chandeliers and vivid colours such as teal and burgundy enlivened with quirky prints. The food will make those who thought nouvelle cuisine the very epitome of the Emperor's new clothes extremely happy - the English Lounge kitchen staff provide hearty dinners indeed. A 2005 *City Life* sampled Roasted wild boar steak (£11.75), for example, came as a large cut sat on a shaped tower of cubed potatoes. It was surrounded by deep, rich and meaty red wine jus and enhanced with glazed and roasted Bramley apples and kumquats. A pudding of Rhubarb, raspberry and redcurrant pastry case, topped with frangipane and apricot glaze (£3.95) was another substantial beast. To look at both dishes provided sensory overload, but they were also robust, filling and good value. Dining partners were a democratic lot - not restricted to foodie middle-classes or professionals on expenses. Cask ales: Timothy Taylor's Landlord - there's a good wine list too. Children: welcome. Disabled access: full.

Mr Thomas's Chop House

52 Cross Street, City

0161 832 2245 5D

www.tomschophouse.com

Thank the Lord, Thomas's is finally going to serve food in the evenings. Young chef Kai Smith's enterprising British-based cuisine is already a lunchtime match for this glorious pub - it was about time he entertained our evening tastebuds too. The Thomas's we see today dates from 1901, when Robert

Walker reworked the older pub on the site. Outside, it is rich brown terracotta and is a Cross Street landmark, despite its modest size. Inside, the pub is long and thin with a handsome wooden bar, sumptuous green tiles and a series of clever receding arches that are so effective they make architects weep for their own inadequacy - or they should. Try anything off the menu - the game, the beef, the fish - and it should satisfy. One of the best dishes in Manchester in 2005 was the Slowly roasted honey coated belly pork, on a bed of caramelised onions with five-spice lentils and apple puree (£11.95). The wine list is generous too, with over 30 choices. Outside to the rear, under the shadow of St Ann's Church is the most handsome and comfortable (no traffic) pub terrace in the city centre by a mile, which features occasional barbeques in summer. Thomas's is a sister establishment to Sam's Chop House (see pg 35). Cask ales: Boddingtons, Black Sheep plus at least one guest ale. Children: welcome before 7pm, now with high chairs for small children.

Belly pork at Mr Thomas's Chophouse

Ox Hotel

71 Liverpool Street, City
0161 839 7740 2F

www.theox.co.uk

After a fallow period in early 2005, the Ox seems to be back on track. The Ox (full name Oxnoble, after a popular 19th century potato, fact fans) combines a traditional pub atmosphere with contemporary culinary flair. The starter of Roasted Mediterranean figs stuffed with buffalo mozzarella and wrapped in Parma ham (£5.95) is a fine example of the place's modern yet hearty fare, as are the Seared Cornish scallops scented with garlic and chilli butter (£6.95) - sure to warm the cockles. For a comforting main course, try the Milk-poached smoked haddock fillet on saffron-

steamed Jersey Royals topped with a poached egg and a light watercress cream (£9.95). There's an impressive range of malts and Irish whiskies, with a recommended wine (often private reserve) for each daily special. Few so-called Northern 'gastro-pubs' retain the ability to seat serious diners next to after-work drinkers, but the Ox is almost a parad-Ox in this respect: the silverware might sparkle and the napkins might be freshly pressed, but look hard enough and you'll still see a shred of sawdust on the floor. Maybe. Cask ale: Black Sheep, Boddingtons, Landlord, Deuchers plus two guests. Children: welcome before 7pm. Disabled access: full.

Suburban pubs

This is the *City Life* choice of the finest pubs away from the city centre. Some are included for their pure brilliance, some for a particular feature and some for their wonderful eccentricity.

City south
The Beech

72 Beech Road, Chorlton
0161 881 1180

Situated at a fine crossroads for character-filled pubs - opposite the Trevor Arms and round the

corner from the Horse and Jockey - and just by Chorlton Green, the Beech is a long way away from the Chorlton image of swanky bars and cafes. And it's all the better for it. With its two smallish rooms, beer garden and - gasp - no food other than peanuts and crisps, this is a textbook traditional pub. There's a nice mix of the trendy and the not-so-trendy, a fine collection of cask ales, and the large beer garden is always packed once the sun comes out. Cask ales: Timothy Taylor's Landlord and Best, Abbot Ale, Marstons Pedigree, Deuchars IPA, Tigar and guests. Children: welcome before 7pm in main building and 9pm in beer garden.

Fletcher Moss

1 William Street, Didsbury
0161 438 0073

Formerly the Albert pub, this is presently very busy with a pleasant interior slightly tarnished by the sort of conservatory you'd find in a suburban garden. This Hydes house avoids being a lagered-up youth club as so many are down these parts. Fletcher Moss was a local councillor, by the way, who donated the nearby Parsonage and Fletcher Moss parks to the locals. A Lancastrian, he once wrote that 'Cheadle folk are good-looking in a Cheshire sort of way but

Out of town

If you want proper gin palaces, head west and sample the delights of the Holt's houses in Eccles.

One of the most interesting mini pub crawls in Greater Manchester can be based around three establishments in Eccles belonging to Manchester brewer Joseph Holt's. It's convenient too. Taking the Metrolink, you can be inside the first of these, the Lamb, within about 20 minutes of leaving the city centre.

All the pubs are Grade II listed and date from a period of wealth and expansion for the Holt family around a century ago. Money without taste, of course, is nothing. Lucky, then, that the boss of Holt's at this time was one of the most discerning Mancs around, Edward Holt (the future Lord Mayor of Manchester). It was he who decided to upgrade several of his pubs in the grandest manner possible.

The Lamb (Regent Street, Eccles, 0161 789 3882) was rebuilt in 1906 (it underwent a minor refurbishment last Christmas, though the extensive French polishing was still going strong during a recent visit - it's a six-month operation) with magnificent Brazilian mahogany, coloured mosaics, delicately etched glass and intricate Art Nouveau tiling. It remains a pub in every sense of the word, with large separate rooms and a snug at the front. No food is served, there is no music whatsoever and no Sky TV - conversation and having a good laugh are the watchwords. Games include darts, dominoes and cards. There's also a full-sized snooker table where all your limitations on the green baize can be explored.

A short taxi ride away is the equally memorable, in both design and atmosphere, **Grapes** (Liverpool Road, Peel Green, Eccles, 0161 789 6971). There's more superb mahogany, glass and tile and be sure to check out the amazing staircase. The Vault features darts, but only of the Manchester variety - different board and no trebles. Once again, only beer drinkers and those looking for conversation are required.

Midway between the two is the **Royal Oak** (Barton Lane, Eccles, 0161 789 0487) from 1904. This has a single bar in the large vault and then service via hatches elsewhere. There's more splendid glass, wood and tile work throughout, with even the original stable block in the back yard.

By the way, one of Edward Holt's private homes is now open for public view - his second home at Blackwell House, near Bowness in the Lake District. The interior by Baillie-Scott is unforgettable, just like the second homes of so many Eccles people 80 miles southeast.

The Lamb

there are still some faces on the high street from which even a well-bred horse will shy'. This info is irrelevant on a visit to this pub, but it's funny don't you think? Cask ales: Hydes Bitter, Mild and Jekyll's Gold plus seasonal ales.

The Metropolitan

2 Lapwing Lane, Didsbury
0161 374 9559
www.the-metropolitan.co.uk
Seemingly all things to all people, the ambition behind this Didsbury big boy cannot be faulted. A sunny day sees the beautiful people take full advantage of the huge outdoor space - with heaters, just in case - while the spacious, yet comfortingly quaint interior is perfect for a winter warmer or three, and in a place this large it's reassuringly easy to lose yourself for an evening. The restaurant may be a little on the expensive side, but it's tasty enough fodder: Escalope of pork with pancetta, emmenthal and tomato salsa is a winner, as is the quite mighty Metropolitan burger - a heavyweight if ever we saw one. Cask ales: Pedigree, Deuchars IPA, Timothy Taylors, Landlord. Children: welcome in bar area until 8pm. Disabled access: full.

The Railway

3 Lapwing Lane, West Didsbury
0161 445 9839

This cosy community pub sits in the heart of West Didsbury opposite the Metropolitan and tends to bottleneck on weekend evenings with the sheer mass of punters. It was, in fact, once Britain's smallest pub, and with sparse seating, the huge table at the back of the room seems to have the same coveted status as the couch in *Friends*. The mixed clientele include older folk who prefer the traditional feel of the pub as well as the influx of university students keen to get a taste of local life. Real ales are on offer, as are guest ales on a regular basis. There's good traditional home cooked food served from Friday to Sunday and on Mondays there's lunch and a curry night. Cask ales: Joseph Holt. Games/ents: quiz every Tuesday evening. Disabled access: partial.

Rampant Lion

Anson Road, Victoria Park

0161 248 0371

Peter Orgill, Simon Cooper and Paul Astill are the fellas behind Cord and Centro bars in the city centre. With the Rampant Lion, they have spread out to the suburbs - or at least to Victoria Park. Inside the impressive shell of a mid-19th century building they have created a contemporary pub full of vigorous colour, good food, Sunday roasts at £6.95 and great music. The result is a popular place with locals and students alike, incorporating a well-used function room. Try it if you're in the area. Cask ales: Old Speckled Hen, Timothy Taylor's Landlord. Games/ents: quiz and student night Rampage on Tuesdays, Unstaged live music on Thursdays, Sound and Vision with the dapper DJ Richard Hector-Jones on Fridays, Monkey Bars with Fat City Records DJs on Saturdays. Children: welcome until 7pm.

West of the city
The Crescent

18/20 The Crescent, Salford

0161 736 5600

www.beerfestival.com/crescent

Winner of the *City Life* Pub of the Year 2004, the Crescent is a fabulous pub first and foremost and then a fabulous real ale house: a perfect place in which to pursue a beery passion but also a damn fine location to just pass the time and chew the cud. There are regular beer festivals in which a startling

array of ales appear, from the lesser known English breweries but also don't miss the Belgian and German beers on draught and the numerous bottled varieties. Good simple food is available, such as Beef in Guinness, a function room is free to hire and there's darts and Sky TV. The whole place is a labyrinth - a warren of rooms that are frankly a mess. For instance, there should be no excuse for that '70s fake half-timbering but somehow, mystically, the Crescent gets away with it. The jukebox has classic tracks including Bob Dylan, The Stranglers and much else. Cask ales: Hyde's bitter, Phoenix Thirsty Moon, Roosters Special, Erdinger, Black Pig Mild, Paulaner, Liefmans Kriek (cherry beer) plus 7 guests including Bazens'. Games/ents: quiz on Mondays, curry night on Wednesdays and those 4 beer festivals a year, showcasing 40 beers over 4 days. Children: daytime during food service hours. Disabled access: partial.

Ashton-under-Lyne
Junction Inn

Mossley Road, Hazlehurst

0161 343 1611

Where can you get good Lancashire,

fill-you-up-to-the-brim rag puddings these days? The Junction's the place, and besides those tasty puds (and roast dinners, home-made pies and so on), there's a lot of other things going for the place. There's the charming stone building itself, with a jumble of small rooms, and there's also the prospect of walks after the puddings, of course. Cask ales: Robinson's range including Hatters, Unicorn and seasonal ales. Children: up to 7pm.

Bolton
Ye Old Man And The Scythe

Churchgate, Bolton

01204 527 267

Eccentric enthusiast John runs this fine and ancient pub with zest and flair, making it an oasis in the Friday-night hell that is Bolton town centre - he claims its one of the oldest in Britain dating back to the 13th century. The pub, with parts from the 1250s, has its own ghosts. For £2 per head, John will take groups on tours - he thinks he's the embodiment of James Cockerel, who was the licensee during the English Civil War. The food is basic: chilli, curry, and soups served in big bowls with bread. Or you can order

Rampant Lion

a Chinese meal from the take-away next door and get it put on a plate here. Games/ents: these are a cut above and include darts, chess, cards, guitar workshop on Mondays, quiz on Tuesdays, club meetings on Wednesdays, clinic with registered healer Adam Atkinson (for people with aches and pains etc - according to the landlord, one regular had her sense of smell restored after nine years without it) on Thursdays, live singalong music from Howard Broadbent (strictly pre-'60s set) 7pm-9.30pm on Fridays, Bolton Acoustic Session for songwriters and open mic performers 7pm-10.30pm on Saturdays. Cask ales: Boddingtons, Holt's, Flowers Original, Flowers IPA, Deuchars. Ciders: Pheasant Plucker, Bulmers Traditional, Thatchers (currently selling over 150 gallons of cider a week). Children: welcome before 7pm. Disabled access: full in main bar and toilets.

Sweet Green Tavern

127 Crook Street, Bolton
01204 392 258

Four small rooms in an old terrace handily close to the station and not so far from the best fish market around. The atmosphere is chatty and easy and there's a lovely unspoilt vault. Simple homely food is served every day from noon to early evening and there's a real fire to take advantage of in the winter months,

and an outdoor drinking area for summer. Cask ales: Tetley bitter plus five guest ales, a mild and a cider. Games/ents: dominoes, cribbage, dart, pool, Kerplunk, backgammon. Children: up to 7.30pm. Disabled access: partial.

Bury
The Trackside

Bolton Road Station, Bury
0161 764 6461

First we had Stalybridge Buffet Bar and now we've got this gem at Bolton Street Station. Not that you are likely to see any passing mainline trains, except retired ones, as this is the head office station for the East Lancs Railway, Greater Manchester's glorious heritage line. The pub is a sweet single space with good, simple food such as Manx kippers or whole Bury black pudding with mustard and piccalilli. Take a trip out, enjoy the old steamers puffing past and settle back with the fine ales. Cask ales: nine real ales, 39 bottled beers. Games/ents: darts room, occasional live entertainment. Cask ales: changing range. Children: welcome until 7pm. Disabled access: full.

Heaton Norris
Nursery Inn

258 Green Lane (off the A6), Heaton Norris
0161 432 2044

Get out the A-Z and find this place. Winner of the CAMRA National Pub of the Year 2001, it is lost down a cobbled lane but once found, proves hugely worthwhile. As the world prepared for war in 1939, this pub prepared to open. It still sports superb and original wood panels and stained glass. Food such as the traditional roast (£5.50) is very popular and there are daily specials and other home cooked foods. The bowling green is equally well kept and well used. Not so far away is the Navigation, another cracking pub that serves Congleton's Beartown range of ales. Cask ales: full range of Hyde's beers plus 1 guest. Games/ents: darts, bowling green, live music on Saturdays occasional live music on Sundays, quiz Mondays, 'Why Worry' folk club meets (people bring own instruments) last Tuesday of the month. Disabled access: full (partial on bowling green).

Middleton
The Old Boar's Head

Long Street, Middleton
0161 643 3520.

With parts dating back to the 14th century, this is a gem of an ancient building and looks it too. Located within a mile or so of Lees brewery, it's no surprise that the company care for this pub is meticulous. The timber-framed building on sturdy stone foundations is an Olde Englande dream. The floor plan of the building seems to have grown organically over time rather than been deliberately constructed by man. There is good pub food available and a large function room for parties, weddings etc. Custom to the latter is no doubt increased by the proximity to Middleton's superb parish church with its Lowryesque view southeast from the adjacent churchyard. Cask ales: JW Lees Bitter, Mild, seasonal Lees beers. Games/ents: quiz night Tuesdays. Children: until 9pm. Disabled access: full.

The Nursery Inn

Tandle Hill Tavern

14 Thornham Lane, Slattocks

07706 345 297

This is hidden away up an unmetalled road in the beautifully titled suburb of Slattocks and is a scruffy gem with odd and unpredictable opening hours. There are two rooms and a real fire, plus home-made soups and snacks. The pub is particularly useful as a watering hole after (or before) visiting the splendid Tandle Hill Country Park above - this provides some of the best views across Greater Manchester into the Pennines. Cask ales: Lees range. Children: welcome.

Rochdale

The Albion

600 Whitworth Road, Healey, Rochdale

01706 648540

A proper pub carved into the Pennines with a crazy rear beer garden on a terrace so steep it's almost on the roof. The Albion is a collection of small rooms with a titchy bar, a real fire, good bar food and an excellent, non-smoking, midnight licensed bistro offering tasty, amply proportioned food that reflects the landlord's South African origins. There are several good theme evenings, such as a gourmet night on the last Friday and a trad South African buffet on the first Tuesday of the month. The extensive wine list has more than 15 wines from South Africa and an impressive range of ports and brandies. The landlord even has his own wine merchant company, RSA Wine Imports (www.rsawineimports.com). Half a mile west is the stone-built Healey Hotel (01706 645453) with petanque piste - popular on Sundays - original 1930s features and Robinson's ales. A mile north is the Birches (01706 344119) with a terrace overlooking the bowling green, Healey Dell,

Stalybridge Buffet Bar

craggy Top O'Pike and the sunset. Cask ales: Taylor's Best, Golden Best and Landlord), JW Lees, Bazens Blue Bullet, Bazens Dark Mild, Moorhouses Blond Witch, Thwaites Lancaster Bomber, Leffe on draught. Children: welcome until 9pm - kids menu. Disabled access: full.

Stalybridge

The Railway Station

Rassbottom Street, Stalybridge

0161 303 0007

www.buffetbar.co.uk

Nominated for *City Life* Manchester Food and Drink Festival Pub of the Year and a wunderbar wonder bar. The shock of finding this place on Platform One is enough to make you break out in lunatic laughter. The joys are manifold, including a huge station clock, real fires, real ales, real builders-size mugs of tea and real black peas - remember to dowse the latter in vinegar. Of course, there's a good range of continental bottled beers as well. This is an award winning pub that has appeared in all the guides. Cask ales: Flowers IPA; Boddingtons, plus 6 guests beers. Games/ents: folk club Saturdays, quiz Monday nights 9pm, beer festivals. Children: welcome before 9pm. Disabled access: full.

Stockport

The Arden Arms

23 Millgate Street, behind Asda, Stockport

0161 480 2185

The Camra North West Pub of the Year 2004. For period detailing and excellence of pub grub, the Arden Arms is well worth the steep walk down from Stockport Parish Church and Market. The building is more or less an original Georgian inn with a real fire as a bonus - the survival of a full 18th century coachyard is now utilised as an outdoor drinking area. The most peculiar interior space is the little snug accessed through the bar servery, and thus a private space for meetings or small groups. The lunchtime food is an added bonus (Monday-Friday noon-2.30pm, Saturday-Sunday noon-4pm). The food is all home made but of restaurant quality and at pub prices. Examples include the popular hot roast beef on ciabatta with caramelised onions, and there are main course specials on offer too. Cask ales: Robinson's range plus seasonal ale. Children: welcome until 6pm. Games/ents: darts and board games, live band every first Sunday of the month, live music occasionally on Tuesdays and Thursdays. Disabled access: partial.

Bells of Peover

Blossoms

2 Buxton Road, Heavily

0161 477 2397

A Victorian lovely, which was originally built as a coaching house and has with five rooms, some in a splendid condition. The back room is the best, with etched window panes and a glorious fireplace. It's a friendly and popular place too, with an excellent jukebox, home-made pies and a celebrity link - if Badly Drawn Boy was ever a celebrity. The be-hatted one liked the place so much he used it for the artwork on his album *One Plus One Is One*, which contains an instrumental track called 'The Blossoms'. Cask ales: Robinson's range, Hatters, Unicorn and Old Tom in winter. Games/ents: pool, darts, quiz Thursday nights. Children: until 7.30pm. Disabled access: partial.

Queens Head

12 Little Underbank, Stockport

0161 480 0725

This superb and atmospheric little survivor is arraigned higgledy-piggledy all over a hillside under the iron bridge of St Peter's Gate. There's a number of features worth noting on a visit, not least the sweet snug that resembles a first class Victorian train compartment. The bar area is lovely, with a full range of period taps. Up the stone stairs is a room, allegedly haunted by the ghost of a cavalier - try to find the chill spot. The pub boasts (if that's the right word) the smallest urinal in England. Daily papers and sandwiches can help delay departure from this must-visit in Stockport. Cask ales: Sam Smiths Old Brewery Bitter, Dark Mild, Sovereign. Children: welcome until 6pm.

Urmston
The Greyhound

Church Road, Urmston

0161 748 2063

www.thegreyhoundflixton.co.uk

This former Beefeater pub has been taken over by city chef Robert Owen Brown and it shows with the improved food quality. Not that traces of the old place aren't still in evidence. Come here for a drink by all means but also excellent food such as the Roast salmon fillet with Morecambe bay shrimps and cockles. Is Urmston the new Bray, what with its culinary citizens Isinglass, rising star of the locally sourced fine food scene, and now the Greyhound? Not quite, but this dog is definitely worth a flutter. Range of guest ales. Children's menu: Will do children's portions.

Fringe pubs

These pubs lie on the edge of the Greater Manchester conurbation or are surrounded by countryside.

Bells of Peover

The Cobbles, Lower Peover, off the B5081 south of Knutsford, Cheshire

01565 722 269

Quaint beyond measure and hidden in the countryside of Cheshire, this is a part of the world that is forever England - even though it is now owned by the Chef & Brewer chain. As if the cobbled thoroughfare, low ceilings and the nearby ancient church of St Oswald's weren't enough, the Bells has a stellar reputation amongst fans of seafood with a huge array of menu options on the large chalk board. A selection of hand-pumped ales round off the experience and there is a solid choice of wines and lagers. Interesting fact: US generals Eisenhower and Patten used to meet here discussing plans for the D-Day landings. History buffs will note that Patton made a serious political gaffe of a speech - citing the Russians as potential worthy global leaders, no less - in what became know as the 'Knutsford incident'. One too many shandys perhaps. Nearby is the Crown, another charming pub with a gooseberry competition in July. Cask ales: Bombadier, Courage Directors, Theakstons. Children: over-14s only after 6pm. Disabled access: full.

Crag Inn

Wildboarclough, five miles southeast of Macclesfield off the A54, Cheshire

01260 227 239

The first time *City Life* tried to get out of Manchester this year to find The Crag Inn for a reappraisal, we got horribly lost and wound up god knows where - possibly the Midlands. As a result, it's safe to say that passing trade is at a minimum for this impressive pub. But seek, fellow traveller, and you will find a 500-year-old converted farmhouse with all the trappings: fire places, real wood beams etc. Locally sourced food and a moderate selection of ales will cheer you up before you and friends take a walk around the hill of Shutlingslow (only 506 metres high but steep with it) where Alan Garner set the end of *The Weirdstone of Brisingamen*. Games/ents: jazz evening every first Sunday of the month April-October. Disabled access: full

Davenport Arms (Thief's Neck)

550 Chester Road, Woodford, Stockport

0161 439 2435

A pub that defines the traditional. All the elements are here in this multi-roomed farmhouse pub on the brink of suburbia and over the road, more or less, from Woodford Aerodome.

The boozer is traditional in more ways than one, as the Hallworth family have been running the sweet place for more than seven decades. Comprised of three rooms, each with a real fire, this is a good place to enjoy the home-cooked lunchtime food (fresh fish a speciality) or simply to slip the shackles of the modern world and disappear in a fug of chat. The conversation is unassisted by background music but assisted by well-kept ales. Cask ales: Robinsons range. Children: welcome, children's play area at the back. Games/ents: darts, regular quiz night (look out for notices). Disabled access: full.

The Oddfellows

73 Moor End Road, Mellor, east of Stockport

0161 449 7826

This moorland three-storey delight makes beauty out of its millstone grit rigour. The emphasis here is on fine foods with fish a feature, including monkfish, snapper and swordfish. There is a satisfying lack of piped music and electronic games, so the only noise is chat and the clink of cutlery on crockery, glass against table. The stone-flagged bar is a delight with its open fires. The surroundings are lovely and worth exploring and there's a pleasant seating area outside. It's not the easiest place to find, in a dip in the road between Marple Bridge and New Mills, but worth the effort. Cask ales: Adnams, Phoenix Arizona, Boddingtons and one guest beer. Children: welcome until early evening. Disabled access: partial (toilets are upstairs).

The Pack Horse

52 Watling Street, Affetside, Near Tottington, Bury

01204 883 802

Affetside is a hamlet with a Saxon name, an ancient cross and one street as straight as a die courtesy

of the Romans. Any dalliance can be assisted by a visit to the excellent local, the Pack Horse - an appropriate title as these beasts have been trooping along the road here for almost 2,000 years. With great views, a family-friendly policy (kids have their own room) and real fires, this is well worth a stop. You might even get a visitation from the ghost of the executioner of Lord Strange in Bolton in 1651 - the man whose skull lies behind the bar. The food is unexceptional but adequate. Cask ales: Hydes beers. Children: welcome until 9pm. Games/ents: pool room plus occasional quiz nights. Disabled access: partial.

The Romper

Ridge End, Marple

0161 427 1354

Perhaps the best feature of this pub is its location with extensive views, whilst a little below to the east is the Peak Forest Canal that provides easy strolls along the towpaths. There are tables outside the Romper to enable customers to enjoy the views in summer. The interior is oak beamed and comfortable with good food, a broad range of wines and a decent selection of malt whiskies. This is a great starting point - or a good lunch break - for walks in the surrounding countryside. Cask ales: Landlord, Bombadier, John Smith. Children: welcome in the restaurant.

Black Dog

Church Street, Belmont, north of Bolton

01204 811 218

Belmont lies on the A675 and is grouped around the four-centuries-old Black Dog pub. This has pleasant seating in front and a pretty courtyard out back. It is a low slung, keep the warmth in type of place split into several rooms with brasses, old prints and banquettes. The menu is extensive and good value with lots

The Cross Keys

of Brit traditionals and also offers dishes with a slight continental drift. Most meals are reasonably priced and fall within the £6-£6.50 mark. The minor road that leads west here to the excellent Rivington Pike climbs over 1,100 feet above sea level and gives views of Blackpool Tower and the Welsh mountains. The pub is a hubbub of activity, with mountain climbing, gardening and even fly fishing clubs holding regular meetings. Cask ales: Joseph Holt's. Disabled access: partial.

Church Inn

Church Lane, Uppermill, Saddleworth, Oldham

01457 820 902

A British classic and eccentricity central. Here's the list of craziness: the once Morris-dancing head brewer of the on-site micro-brewery is no longer, although the group still practise outside the pub on summer weekends; the collar on the wall is used for gurning over August Bank Holiday; the handbells on display are the local bell ringers' training set; outside in the imbibing area facing the moors, you can find a menagerie of geese, rabbits and horses etc. What more could you ask for? Seek it out. There's good food too: everything from bar snacks through to cheap mains of duck, gammon

and pasta. If you really like the pub, you can stay forever - on-site grave plots are available. Cask ales: Saddleworth More, Hop Smacker and Shaft Bender, plus 3/4 guests, Saxon homebrew cider and malt whiskies. Children: welcome before 9pm. Games/ents: the pub itself is the entertainment, otherwise unplugged evenings on Fridays and live bands on Saturdays. Function rooms available.

Cross Keys

Running Hill Gate, Uppermill, Saddleworth, Oldham

01457 874 626

From cottage industry for textiles to superb hill pub in a couple of centuries. This strong pub sits squarely on the hills and gives easy access to the natural craggy wonders of the Pots and Pans above Greenfield. Any weather will do, but the extremes are best here - a sunny summer's day for the excellent beer garden or a raging storm coming in off the moor with the Cross Keys as the dream refuge. And you'll know you're safe, because a mountain rescue team is based across the road. The interior is just what you would wish for: a real fire, stone flagging and a huge cooking range providing good pub food, which is served both in the afternoon and during the evening on weekdays and all day at weekends. It's a family-friendly pub and the ample beer garden has children's play area with climbing frames and the like. Cask ales: full range of JW Lees beers including the kickass Moonraker at 7%. Children: welcome until 9pm. Also very community orientated, with over 20 clubs and societies that meet there, including Manchester Pedestrians (who've been walking for over 100 years - they must be tired) and Saddleworth Running Club. Games/ents: folk music Wednesday/Sunday nights 8.30pm. Disabled access: partial.

Lord Raglan

Mount Pleasant, Nangreaves, Bury

0161 764 6680

www.leydenbrewery.com

The up and down, side to side motion is intriguing to begin with. But after more than half a mile, it gets alarming. Then, 40 miles from the coast, and with the onset of seasickness, the Lord Raglan makes a timely appearance. Is its approach road the longest remaining cobbled lane in Lancashire? The pub itself is also caught in a time warp, this time from around 1978 - with brasses and hunting horns, grandfather clocks and Welsh dressers. It's an expanded version of your gran's front room but with lots of alcohol. And it's the booze that the Raglan does best, with a decent range of malt whiskies and its on-site micro-brewery, the Leyden Brewery, providing six or more ales. The food, despite the big restaurant part, is seldom better than okay. Cask ales: the Leyden range - if it's on try the delicious Black Pudding mild. Children: welcome.

Pack Horse Inn

Off B6222, Elbut Lane, Birtle, nr Bury

0161 764 3620

Hiding away on the hills between Rochdale and Bury is this classic stone-built moorland pub from the 18th century. It's got a classic interior too, with horse brasses, copper pots, grandfather clocks, real fires, the works. The new conservatory allows drinkers and diners to take in the views over the fields. The two tiny snugs here provide an added escape from the noise and clutter of the daily round. The adjacent barn has been converted into a restaurant serving good food. Cask ales: JW Lees range. Children: very welcome. Disabled access: full.

Royal Oak (Th'Heights)

Broad Lane, Heights (above Denshaw Road), Delph

01457 874460

Just as you are leaving Delph on the A6052, there's the tiniest of minor roads on your right. Follow this to the Heights and the lovely Royal Oak pub. There are great views over Grains Bar southwest to the Greater Manchester conurbation. The beer is good and the food can be excellent. But the star of the show is the multi-roomed intimate interior, which is strong, simple and plain - the antithesis to any themed pub nonsense. The best way to arrive is on foot from Delph - this gives the added frisson of walking back down in the black night past the eerie church. And there are three open fires to warm the cockles if you've walked there. Food is very good and all home cooked with plenty of game. All beef is Scottish beef. Cask ales: Black Sheep best bitter and usually Phoenix, Millstone and guests. Children: welcome until 9pm. Disabled access: partial.

Strawbury Duck

Overshores Road, Entwistle, north of Bolton

01204 852 013

One Friday evening you should leave work, go to Victoria Station with your paramour, take the train to Entwistle Station and stay over in the Strawbury Duck. 25 minutes from town and you're out in the hills with a wholesome meal, a good range of drinks and friendly locals with whom to share the bar. And outside, there's a cobbled courtyard in which to take advantage of long summer evenings. Food is decent, covering the bases from sandwiches to mains - you could also dip into the frequently less homely choice of 11 specials posted on the blackboard. And if you can't stay over, the last train to Victoria is conveniently at 11.20pm. There's a beer garden with pergola at the front and some seating out back. Cask ale: Boddingtons, Landlord, Pendle Witch and Black Sheep normally, with two guests, malt whiskies and 20 wines. Children: welcome. Disabled access: partial.

Swan Inn (Top House)

1 The Square, Dobcross, Saddleworth

01457 873 451

Dobcross is a wonderful stone Pennine village. If you've not been there yet, it's time to visit. You might even find a touch of the familiar, as the village was a key location in the Richard Gere movie *Yanks*. The Swan fits perfectly into his quaint chocolate box charm. The pub has flagged floors, a function room and gets rammed during the Rushcart Festival in August and during the Whit Friday brass band contests. There is a real fire and no music. The building has the dubious honour of having been built for the Wrigleys, a Saddleworth family who eventually emigrated and started the chewing gum giant. Here you can enjoy real ale and good home-cooked grub

such as chicken tikka and lamb shank plus 20 specials - book ahead on weekends. Cask ales: full range of Jennings cask ales (6 in total), the only place around with them, and 2 guest ales. Games/ents: folk jam session from 9pm on Thursdays, rhythm and blues night every other Sunday. Children: welcome until 9.30pm. Disabled access: full

The White House

A58, Blackstone Edge, Littleborough, nr Rochdale

01706 378 456

Perched high on the harshly beautiful Pennine Way, the White House is the last pub in Lancashire before you head for Yorkshire a quarter of a mile away. If you stop and eat here, you will memorably savour the experience as you trudge on. This is a large old coaching house that dates from 1671, and is a former haunt for the young bloods of Littleborough who valiantly guarded the mail coach from the perils of pouncing highwaymen. The views from here are breath taking and the food is very good too. Cask ales: Theakstons Bitter, Black Sheep plus 2 guests. Children: welcome until 9pm. Disabled access: partial.

The White House

Coffee bars & food shopping

Coffee shops and cafes

Deansgate around the Queen Street junction has gone coffee mad, with Starbucks and Caffè Nero on one side and Eat on the other. There's hardly enough gap to squeeze a skinny latte through. Mancunians must be working too hard and staying up too late to need all this coffee. The sad thing is that all these arrivals are part of international or national chains. But don't despair: if you hanker for something a little more unusual, that's what this section is for, so you won't find another mention of the S-word. As embodied by the *City Life* Coffee Bar of the Year 2005, Suburb, individuality courses through this chapter like an espresso through the bloodstream.

Barton Aerodrome

Off the A57, two miles west of Eccles

0161 789 1866

This is here for the curiosity value, serving basic stewed teas and instant coffees plus soft drinks and some snacks. Indeed you don't visit here for quality nosh, but for its oddness, with the enthusiasts' museum and small grassed area. This is the only place where you can sip your tea and get your hair blow dried - by an ascending

helicopter. For those who love aviation, eccentrics should also try the Manchester Airport Viewing Area - follow signs off the A538 for the mobile café.

Battery Park

615a Wilbraham Road, Chorlton

0161 860 0754

With Battery Park, the key to any visit is the high quality of the juices, smoothies and shakes - some of which, it is claimed, can help dispel hangovers. BP also has a range of snacks, home-made cakes, pastries, sandwiches, baked potatoes, home-made soups and coffee. There is some summer seating outside and art exhibitions in the back room.

Chinese Arts Centre

Market Buildings, Thomas Street, City

0161 832 7271 8B

www.chinese-arts-centre.org

A beautiful light and airy design from Omi architects and a joy to visit. The tea house offers a broad selection of teas to sample and take home too. Tuck into green, black, oolong, white, yellow, red, flower or compressed tea - this last is also known as brick tea to ease transportation and storage and can be stored for decades without significantly deteriorating. Amidst the activity and change in the Northern Quarter, the tea house provides a moment of tranquillity.

Diamond Dogs

52 Beech Road, Chorlton

0161 882 0101

Veggie restaurant or coffee bar? Well there's definitely more of a café feel to this place with its DIY Bowie inspired chic punk décor. A choice of three soups for starters

are balanced by a choice of three desserts, all of which are varieties of cheesecake. Yet aside from the typical nut roast fare, you're bullied into either the not-so-green Thai green curry or the Spinach and parmesan quiche. Still, Diamond Dogs has an adventurous range of frothy smoothies and fruit juices plus a programme of art exhibitions/ poetry readings/ live music. It's heart seems in the right place.

Fitzpatrick's Herbal Health

5 Bank Street, Rawtenstall

01706 211 152

115-year-old Fitzpatrick's is Britain's last temperance bar. The drinks are made on the premises, served hot or cold and dispensed from ceramic kegs. Visitors can indulge in dandelion and burdock, blood tonic and black beer among others. A proper crowd-pleaser is the ginger beer, which has world's greatest kick-ass hit of ginger at the back of the throat. Meanwhile, the bar's sarsaparilla is a real winner, not just because of its complex earthy flavour but also because in a national competition in April, it came out as the UK's top dog in a blind tasting. Talk about a stiff drink too - according to the staff, sarsaparilla has the properties of Viagra. Expect an email any minute now encouraging you to 'prolong the experience and make her happy with sarsaparilla'. Most drinks are 50p a half pint, £1 a pint. Bottles of cordial, or neat drinks to take away, cost between £2.50 and £2.99. The drinks are the main event but the bar also stocks row upon row of glass jars packed with valerian, wormwood, raspberry leaf and so on. Each has its own use - valerian, for example, relaxes the nerves, is good for headaches and aids sleep. You can also get homeopathic remedies in more modern packaging, including the romantically titled 'Aloe Vera colon cleanse' - the perfect gift for that special someone, perhaps. As a final flourish, Fitzpatrick's carries a wide range of old-fashioned boiled sweets in big jars such as Everton mints.

Fletcher Moss Park Café

Wilmslow Road, Didsbury

0161 434 1877

This place is all about situation and cakes. The view from the terrace of the delightful rock gardens is one of the sweetest in the region. The cakes here - best enjoyed al fresco on a summer's day - are home-made delights. It's important too, in that wonderful Manchester radical way: the café building hosted a meeting of local ladies in 1890 from which the Royal Society for the Protection of Birds derived. Opening times can be unpredictable on weekdays and in winter.

Katsouris

Deansgate, City

0161 819 1260 5D

Bury Market based Katsouris has opened a daytime deli-café and immediately made an impact. The meaty and veggie hot sandwiches here (ciabattas, baps and so on) are gorgeous - ten times better than Subway's banality. Take the Spicy chorizo ciabatta (£2.20-£2.50) with onions and fried onion. This is just what you want from a great lunchtime sandwich, a sturdy assemblage of flavour-packed wallop. There's bratwurst and meatloaf choices amongst others too. In fact, whilst viewing the queue for these delights, you might find that everything goes shimmery and man and woman alike turn into salivating Homer Simpsons about to say, "Mmm… bratwurst baps". The presentation at Katsouris is another bright point, the highlight being the hanging hams over a good cold meat counter with Barbakan-

Love Saves the Day

46-50 Oldham Street, City

0161 832 0777 9C

www.lovesavestheday.co.uk

Also 345 Deansgate, City

0161 834 2266 3G

This exemplary Manchester independent bistro, coffee shop and deli is a previous *City Life* Coffee Bar of the Year award winner and winner of the Manchester Pioneers Award 2004. Now in splendid new premises, LStD is still leading the way, making the northern end of Oldham Street a real daytime destination. With its 7pm closing time Mondays to Saturdays (4.30pm Sundays), it also hosts various events and tastings. Along with the usual range of coffee choices, cappuccinos etc, there's the in-house Northern Quarter blend and around ten different herbal and traditional teas. The enterprising and daily specials menu covers the ground

between soups and mains and on to desserts with typical LStD élan. Presentation boxes and hampers for Valentine's and Christmas and so on are good value and imaginative. The Deansgate branch also has a small attached cafe. Both outlets provide attractive space for the retail side of the operation. The Deansgate branch provides particularly handsome retailing, with shelves scraping the ceiling and the deli counter providing staples such as olives, fancy breads and pasta. The wines, many of interesting Italian provenance, are a real speciality. Some things you should know about LStD: you never have a bad coffee, salad, Spanish omelette or quiche, and there has never been a poor wine recommendation. You can also trust them to have their heart in the right place when it comes to local produce as well, with proprietor Becky Joyce stocking good local chutneys, cheeses and hams and so on. The Red Room at the Oldham Street site is a good place for a meeting.

Coffee, tea and temperance

Our predecessors had some curious beliefs about coffee, often with reference to its effect on our love lives. In 1674 a group of London lasses petitioned the Mayor to have coffee banned. They wrote that Englishmen had been the 'ablest performers in Christendom' but now 'the abominable, heathenish liquor called Coffee [had] dried up their Radical Moisture... leaving them with nothing stiff but their joints.' The document goes on most saucily to plead for a ban 'so that our Husbands... no more shall run the hazard of being cuckol'd by Dildos.' In fact a recent medical report says, au contraire, although coffee does nothing for the sex life, it does agitate sperm to fertilise eggs faster. Careful of being asked back for coffee.

Rulers of empires and nations had their doubts about the brew too. Ottoman Sultan Murad IV thought that the befuddlement of wine led to contentment in a regime, whereas clear-headed coffee promoted debate and sedition. He took to wandering the streets in well-attended disguise lopping off the heads

of caffeine addicts. Our Charles II banned coffee for the same reason in 1675 - although maybe it was because this most licentious of monarchs was worried by the words of the London women's petition above. But it was too late, the love of coffee was so ingrained that Charles had to withdraw the measure in 11 days.

Tea was attacked for other reasons. It was seen as an effeminate drink, unlike manly beer. In 1757 James Hanway, curiously remembered as the first man to carry an umbrella, attacked it as 'an epidemical disease... You may see labourers who are mending the road drinking their tea.... were they the sons of tea-sippers who won the fields of Crecy and Agincourt?' Tea, thought Lord Brougham, did not contribute to the cultivation of a single English acre whereas beer was 'a moral species of beverage, patriotic, un-French, un-Papist.' Sidney Smith asked, 'what two ideas are more inseparable than beer and Britannia?' whilst Manchester brewer Henry Boddington, perhaps unsurprisingly, stated that 'tea is a dangerous stimulant.' Drink beer, he advised, adding no doubt sotto voce, 'my beer, of course.'

Perhaps we should forget them all and recall the humble words from Boltonian teetotallers 100 years ago. Detox with God's own brew - altogether now, in piety sing, 'I'm very fond of a social glass/ but it must be filled with water./ Water pure doth brighter shine/ than brandy, rum or sparkling wine.'

supplied bread to the right. There's a good selection of meats and breads, but the cheese is pre-packed and limited whilst the overall range of exotic potted, bottled and packaged products is insufficient. The coffee is not spectacular either, but Katsouris is easy to forgive because of those lovely baps...

Manchester Art Gallery Café

Mosley Street, City

0161 235 8888 6E

This is airy on one side, and more loungey with soft seating round the corner. Good soups, salads, cakes and good little lunch boxes for the kids are on offer. This has been the case for many years, and remains so. All in all, it's a great meeting place in the heart of the city with an ace art gallery attached.

Manchester Cathedral Refectory

Cathedral Visitors Centre, Hanging Ditch, City

0161 835 4030 6B

www.manchestercathedral online.co.uk

The Refectory at the Cathedral Visitors Centre makes for an interesting visit and a coffee in itself. It was *City Life* Coffee Bar of the Year in 2002 and is everything a good-quality, old-fashioned teashop should be with the added bonus of an on-site ancient monument, in the form of the double arched 1400s Hanging Bridge. The clean and crisp interior sports an open kitchen providing a range of sandwiches, crusty pies, cakes, tarts, scones, coffee, some speciality teas and even beer and wine. Main course offerings include many seasonal and traditional dishes, such as hot pots and tasty chicken and mushroom pie.

Manna NEW

1 Piccadilly Gardens, City

0161 236 3230 8D

Manna's open plan interior feels light, fresh and airy. With clean slate floors and smatterings of grey and beige, this is an ideal place for a quick snack and a chill-out. Enthusiastic staff serve a variety of organic soups, sandwiches and salads - prices start at £2.05. Manna also caters for a variety of vegetarian and vegan tastes - the vegetarian breakfast at £6 is delicious. Specialities include home-made ice creams and seasonal smoothies from £2. Coffee starts from £1.50 and customers can choose from a range of organic, soya and rice milks.

Oklahoma

Midland Hotel – The Octagon Lounge

Peter Street, City

0161 236 3333 5F

Do tea the classic way in the stately Edwardian surroundings of the exquisite Octagon at the Midland. The set afternoon tea (or coffee, £15.95, 2.30pm-5pm, booking advisable) is served with sandwiches, cakes, scones with clotted cream and preserves and a complementary Madeira wine, or you could sample a rich glass of hot chocolate. It's a great place to charm the grandparents, especially at weekends, or merely to daydream delusions of grandeur upon one's existence. Expect to be serenaded by a pianist 7pm-10.30pm Monday-Saturday.

Oklahoma

14-16 High Street, City

0161 834 1136 8B

Winner of the *City Life* Bar of the Year 2003 and an absolute original with good coffees, smoothies, toasties and light meals. The chairs and couches will be some of the oddest you've ever sat upon and the crowd inside will be cross-section of the Northern Quarter's bohemian best. The coffee bar shares space with the craziest collection of kitsch you'll ever wish to see, which is perfect for stocking fillers and more substantial presents - hula skirt table cloth, Dalek condiment pots or spray-on gay, anyone? There's a superb range of wind-up toys for the child in you as well. Pelicaneck record store also shares space with Oklahoma, providing a trippy, trancey background. Go chill.

Redhouse Farm Tea Rooms and Farm Shop

Redhouse Lane, Dunham Massey, Altrincham

0161 941 3480

www.redhousefarm.co.uk

These tearooms, situated in a former heifer unit in the grounds of National Trust property Dunham Massey, are a breath of fresh air to blow away the city blues. Boasting a 'farmhouse taste', the menu is classic tearoom fodder, and includes various sandwiches, filled baked spuds, a ploughman's lunch, quiche or a simple beans on toast. Finish off with a home-made cake, gateau or the popular apple pie. It's good for the kids too. The attached shop is wonderful for good - usually British - farm-fresh produce.

Rice NEW

Piccadilly Gardens, City 8D

Minimalist and bold, Rice boasts an impressive culmination of black leather bar stools and funky modern tables. On first impressions, it doesn't appear to be your typical take-away, although the emphasis is still on fast dining. Mains on offer include Thai rice stick noodles (£5.49) and Thai fishcakes (£2.99), which are prepared from fresh right before your eyes whilst you wait. A mixture of Indian, Japanese and Thai cuisines, Rice seems to follow in the trend of other Asian restaurant/bars that seem to be popping up across the city. Letss hope it is bold and advantageous enough to stay.

Royal Exchange

Entrances upstairs from Cross Street and Exchange Street (St Ann's Square), City

0161 833 9333 6C

Rain or shine, this is the most impressive interior space in the city to sip on your herbal infusion or snaffle a Danish (you can even down a pint). The coffee shop/bar is located within the great hall of the Royal Exchange - once the main trading room for 80% of all the world's finished cotton trade. The three-coloured glass domes over the theatre provide a changing quality of light as the day wears on. Sample the reasonably priced sandwiches, coffees or the soup of the day. There is a craft shop, bookshop and a more formal restaurant on site too.

Slattery

197 Bury New Road, Whitefield

0161 767 9303

www.slattery.co.uk

Winner of the *City Life* Coffee Bar of the Year 2004 and a wet dream for bon viveurs. Slattery is not only a superb coffee shop and tearooms (with decent wines too) but also one of the North's premier chocolatiers. Aside from a good range of snacks, sandwiches and meals, there are more than 40 varieties of exquisitely sculpted chocolates plus gateaux, desserts and puddings. There's even a bespoke service in larger cakes. Slattery will sculpt anything you want - from novelties such as a wedding scene with a tipsy mother-in-law, to in-house classics such as the glorious Orangina. Proprietor John Slattery has published his own book, *Chocolate Cakes For Weddings and Celebrations*. Another offshoot is the Slattery School of Excellence for those, amateur and professional, who wish to unravel the mysteries of the chocolatier.

Shlurp NEW

2 Brazennose Street Albert Square, City

0161 839 5199 5D

It's soup for the soul in this award winning soup specialist bar. If the friendly banter and spontaneous song from the self-proclaimed three stooges won't warm you, a belly full of wholesome soup will. With a whistle-while-you-work philosophy, these boys ladle up organic and vegetarian soup such as carrot, suede and sweet potato, and spicy chickpea. Delicate, creamy smoked haddock chowder boasts loads of flavour. If meat is more your meal, a steak and kidney casserole with suet pastry crust, or a 'Manchester Floater' of thick pea soup with lamb kofta meatballs and mint will do the trick. Stuffed bagels, wraps and ciabattas are also on the menu, as well as salads such as wild rice, lentils, carrots and orange, and a selection of hot and cold drinks. Knock on the doors at breakfast for home-made porridge and brown sugar. Schlurrp soup on the run, at the counter by the hubbub of the kitchen, or dine outside under the outdoor heaters adjacent to St Mary's Church. But don't forget to say grace.

Soup Kitchen NEW

Spear Street (off Stevenson Square), City

0161 236 5100 9C

The Soup Kitchen was nominated for *City Life* Manchester Food and Drink Festival Coffee Shop of the Year 2005 for its practical, no-nonsense approach to good food and for the cool crowd it attracts. Part of the same business as the nearby Bay Horse (see pg 101), it differs from its compadre in being plainness personified, a concatenation of chipboard with bench seats and low tables. Service is canteen method, with food such as tomato and basil soup, spinach and feta puff pastry, beef kebabs and so on all at bargain prices - a maximum of around £4. A morning and lunchtime venue only, this is a clever addition to Manchester's light meal options.

Suburb

63 Deansgate, City

0161 832 3642 5C

Shlurp

Raise your coffee cups, as Suburb is winner of the *City Life* Coffee Bar of the Year Award 2005. Across the road from some of the more predictable bars in the country and not far from a host of carbon copy coffee shops, this is a model independent - the sort of place you'd want to open if coffee shops were your thing. The coffee is the best in Manchester and the atmosphere relaxed in that easy, leftfield, creative way. Other drinks include Moby's New York Teany range of loose leaf tea in a teapot, Innocent smoothies and so on. And fill your belly with muffins, pastries, ciabattas, paninis, wraps, sticks, bagels, baps and bloomers. There's a select range of CDs to adorn your home collection. Rather than tearing staff away from coffee-making duties to hear the tunes, you can listen at the iPod bar. Bring in your laptop for free internet and downloads with wi-fi, or keep it traditional with a paper and a chat. Note the design of the place: a Victorian shop, dragged into the 21st century with distressed walls, tin tiles on the ceiling and a magnificent full-height sash window. One of the best places in town to get lost is the basement lounge - so good you might only want to come up for that excellent coffee. Register on www.suburbstore.com and you'll get updated on new music releases plus a password for when you can bob in and get a free tea and coffee.

Suburb

Victoria Station and Oxford Road Station Buffet Bars

City
6A and 6G

Grim as can be for food and beverages, but worth a visit for the designs of these places. The first is a phantasmagoria of an Edwardian dome and decorations - it's the place where swags and garlands go to die. Be sure to check out the florid golden mosaic signs of the external walls of the café too. For a change in station mood, another classic is the sweet laminated timber curves of the 1960s Oxford Road station buffet bar - it makes everything IKEA look substandard and cheap.

The Titchy Coffee Company NEW

The Triangle, Exchange Square, City
0161 835 1540

A good little indie café cum coffee shop in amongst the chain retailers of the Triangle. The Titchy Coffee Company provides a happy arrangement of blue and red chairs scattered around the central basement space of the shopping centre under that farcical pod that houses Caffè Nero. Proprietors John Barlow and Claire Vickers have applied great care in sourcing good products. For instance, why bother with a French brie when Cheshire producer Ravens Oak can give you something as lovely as their Burland Green? Or why even consider other types of bread when the organic Barbakan deli is a mere three miles away. The jacket potatoes and sandwiches are very good too, as is the vigorous fairtrade coffee - or you could try Cheshire apple juice instead.

V2Go

Arndale Centre, City
0161 839 8878 6C

An enterprising little number in an unlikely location, with vegetarian food to take away not in the Northern Quarter or Chorlton but in the Arndale. The formula here is simple: quality, freshly prepared, vegetarian food from V dogs (vegetarian hot dogs) via Mexican bean burgers to falafels. Not strictly a café but we had to fit it somewhere. Also in the Trafford Centre.

Zest

9 Gateway House, Piccadilly Station, Approach
0161 236 5252 10E

A very good indie with a breezy modern design, Zest has just about the cheapest good quality coffees in the city centre. Organic fairtrade coffee is also available, along with excellent freshly squeezed juices, wheatgrass and smoothies - the latter standing on their own without space-wasting ice. Also soups, sandwiches, bagels, take out meals and a self-service salad bar. Zest is an example to all would-be independent coffee shops.

Food shopping

The following pages give a brief insight into where to take your wicker basket when the big supermarkets get boring. Of course, the problem is that most of us mean to patronise that little local food provider, but then when it comes down to it we conveniently forget. The shops given here are worth remembering when we need a tastebud boost. No food shopping experience would be complete without a visit to **Chinatown** (but also try the Chinese supermarkets: **Tai Pan**, Upper Brook Street, and **Wing Yip**, Cassidy Close, off Oldham Road, 1km from Piccadilly) and to the **Asian grocers** on Wilmslow Road, Rusholme; Ayres Road, Old Trafford; Cheetham Hill Road, Cheetham Hill; Milkstone Road, Rochdale and along the A6 through Longsight and Levenshulme.

Barbakan Deli

67-71 Manchester Road, Chorlton

0161 881 7053

This 41-year-old was winner of the Manchester Food and Drink Festival 2004 Best Food and Drink Retail Outlet and is extremely popular. The queues are so long on Saturdays that you might want to take a book - *War and Peace* perhaps. Still, it's more than worth the wait. This place has 30-plus types of bread on offer with a new addition in 2005 of sturdy but delicious Chorlton sourdough. There's also a range of traditional deli foods from countries such as Poland (the name of the shop comes from part of the fortifications of Cracow), Italy, Germany and so on, complemented by the best of British. In the last few years, these have been reinforced by a splendid assortment of prepared dishes, salads, sandwiches, teas, coffees and juices. You can snack inside on the high stools or outside on the terrace.

1. Norlander rye bread

2. French campagrain

3. 100% fine rye bread

4. Four-piece bread

5. Polish style black bread

6. Toscana bread

7. Roast potato and rosemary bread

8. Cheese, bacon and tomato bread

Belgian Belly
514 Wilbraham Road, Chorlton
0161 860 6766
www.belgianbelly.com
These people are Low Country crazy. They've got a big reputation too, coming joint runners-up, just a few first months after opening, for the *City Life* Coffee Bar of the Year Award 2003. There's outdoor seating, indoor seating and now a licence for drinking Belgian nectar on the premises. The nectar might be one of over 50 beers, including rare and sublime brews such as Oud Beersel Gueuze (6% abv), Orval Trappist ale (6.2%), Rodenbach Flemish red ale (5%), and the Witkap Stimulo (6%) blond east Flanders ale - then again, you might want to take the things home instead. Another good choice might be the Chocolate Meltdown, delicious hot chocolate plus a selection of six hand-made chocs (£5, £6.95 for two cupfuls). The range of Stephane Dumon chocolates, perfect for presents, is fabulous and includes cerrisettes: a whole cherry soaked in kirsch, with fresh kirsh added then dipped in dark Belgian chocolate. Grub includes Stoovlees - beef braised in Belgian beer with onions and thyme.

Cheese Hamlet
706 Wilmslow Road, Didsbury
0161 434 4781
Some people live their lives by cheese, disclaiming its life enhancing virtues to all who listen. The Cheese Hamlet, as its name suggests, specialises in the wondrous stuff. Expect a busy and colourful interior stacked to the rafters with goodies, with centre stage taken by exotic European cheeses and great classic British cheeses plus veggie options. But there's more - including home cooked meats, fresh pasta, conserves, etc.

Cheshire Smokehouse
Vost Farm, Morley Green, Wilmslow
01625 548 499
Shop and café beloved of in-the-know locals and more than worth the 40-minute or so drive from central Manchester. Cheshire Smokehouse is one of those places where you just know good things are happening. The stock here includes a celebrated range of products prepared on site, such as dry-cured bacon and hams, smoked fish and charcuterie products.

Deli King
Kings Road, Prestwich
0161 798 7370
Deli King remains a superior provider of kosher foods to the UK's second largest Jewish community. This is a handsome place inside and out with a gorgeous period canopy. The mouth-watering selection of foods includes bagels, Israeli-made vegetarian dishes, pickled dishes, exclusive poultry and kosher Indian and Chinese dishes. Supervised by the Manchester Beth Din, its popularity isn't restricted to the Jewish community.

Eazy Cuizine NEW
King Street, Knutsford
0800 542 4727
Ready-made food. Help: that phrase usually stands alongside other foodie words such as 'reconstituted' or 'rehydrated', which means you are sacrificing flavour for convenience whilst slowly poisoning yourself with various chemical reductions. Eazy Cuisine might provide a ready-made alternative, though, as it uses local, quality ingredients where possible and banish all modifiers, stabilisers, artificial colourings, preservatives and additives. The range of products is broad, from soups and sauces to trad British dishes, Med food, curries and game to puddings and hampers. Nothing can compete with good, fresh cooking but if you have to go down the ready-made path, Eazy Cuizine stands out a mile. The products can be bought direct from the shop in Knutsford or by mail order.

Hang Won Hong
58-60 George Street, City
0161 228 6182 7E
Supermarket shopping is generally a bleak and soulless pursuit, unless you're in Hang Won Hong in China Town where thrice-weekly deliveries from Thailand ensure it's brimming with goodies from the Orient. An array of fresh fruit, vegetables and a stack of herbs (fresh and dried), including much sought after Thai basil and a fragrant mound of star anise, wrestle for your attention in this warren of eastern foods. Oodles of noodles and popular delicacies such as liver sausage and instant jellyfish can be topped off with Shaosing rice wine, while typical Chinese sweets and snacks are perfect for nibbling. Kit yourself out for a culinary adventure with their range of Chinese crockery, cutlery and cooking utensils from spits to bamboo steamers. Gawp at or pick out your own live lobster or crab and sample a genuine Chinese pot noodle, the latter regrettably tasting no better than the Knorr alternative.

Ho's Bakery
44-46 Faulkner Street, City
0161 236 8335 7E
If you find yourself roaming Chinatown and are in need of a snack, seek out this fantastic little place. Wander in and you're confronted by scrumptious buns and eccentrically decorated cakes. Whether you're craving something sweet or savoury, the mouth-watering wares here are laid out for your perusal. Everything is baked

within the shop and you can choose from pork dumplings, sweet melon cakes or pick from a selection of pasties including pork, seafood and chicken curry. Their honey buns have achieved legendary status in the city - just ensure you ask for a warm one.

Harvey Nichols

New Cathedral Street, City

0161 828 8898 5B

A smart shop with an upmarket selection of delicacies such as wild boar prosciutto, quails eggs and caviar. There are also prized sausages, bacon, ale, a fresh fruit and veg section (selected by the restaurant chefs) and elusive banana shallots. Cheese lovers can celebrate North West award winners and for hams, try a fantastic Cumbria Mature Royal prepared with a 200-year-old molasses recipe. Sample artichoke hearts, vegan-friendly pesto, dipping oils and sweeties galore - mostly organic.

Olive Delicatessen

Regency House, 36 Whitworth Street, City

0161 236 2360 8F

A bright and colourful deli cum coffee shop with much of what is offered of the standard deli-licious fare. This includes organic foodstuffs, herbs, spices, a range of sandwiches, toasties, bagels and salads to eat in or take away. The alcoholic beverage section is worth a look too.

Roma Delicatessen

268 Bury New Road, Whitefield

0161 766 2941

Behind the standard facade there is a goodie-brimming interior boasting every type of foodstuff necessary to make the perfect Italian meal, such as olives, olive oils, sauces, pasta, cheeses and Italian hams

Inshore Fisheries

Arndale Centre Market, City / 484 Wilbraham Road, Chorlton

0161 881 8353

Inshore is a local company run by a pair with a very fishy background. Their grandfathers before them being fishmongers too, it seems inevitable that these boys have more than just a passing passion for all things slimy and scaly. Inshore was only passed to the capable hands of the current owners two

years ago, but a fishmongers has stood in this spot for 50 years. As a supplier of some of Manchester's finest restaurants, Inshore's superior reputation is citywide. Also providing a good line in rabbit, venison, and other game, even haggis, just ask and these boys will do their best to get it for you. Plaice, monkfish, turbot and herring: anticipate both the usual and more unusual and don't expect the display of seafood to always be the same, what's available depends on what's been hauled in over previous days.

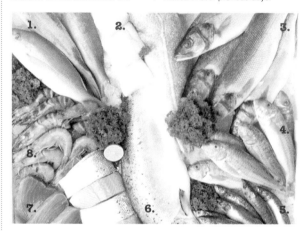

1. Red snapper (£9.95 kilo): Plucked from the North Atlantic in Senegal. Fantastic stuffed with parsley, lemon and thyme.

2. Cod (£12.50): A firm favourite. Only quality mature cod are landed in Fleetwood and Aberdeen. Grill and eat with samphire (marsh grass) and lemon butter.

3. Wild seabass (£10.95 kilo): Bake whole or filleted in a tinfoil parcel with lemon, olive oil and a dash of white wine. Caught in the Fylde.

4. Red Mullet (£9.92 kilo): Cornish dayboat red mullet from Newlyn. Baked whole or steamed with ginger and garlic for an Oriental touch.

5. Sardines (£4.99 kilo): Forget the tinned type. From Cornwall, these slender, oily fish are tasty stuffed with pine kernels and grilled.

6. Organic salmon (£11.95 kilo): Far less greasy and paler fleshed thanks to their organic diet, these salmon come all the way from the isle of Benbecula in Scotland.

7. Tuna (£4.50): Far more flavoursome than the canned alternative. Of such high quality it can be eaten raw. Great flaked over a salad, griddled or barbequed.

8. Crevettes (£10.50 kilo): These crevettes come in all shapes and sizes and are sourced from the Mediterranean.

and meats. A special treat is their scrumptious and award-winning ice cream. They also bake their own bread, which is good enough to justify a trip in its own right. Behind the deli is the café, which offers good value food and drink.

Unicorn Grocery

89 Albany Road, Chorlton

0161 861 0010

Winner of the 2004 Best Provision for Vegetarians at the Manchester Food and Drink Festival - for the second time. The survival and expansion of Unicorn in 2003 is a remarkable story. Threatened by a redevelopment of their building, the Unicorn co-operative asked for support - in pledges and cash - from their appreciative audience. The money flowed in and shortly after, the survival of the North's, and one of Europe's, largest vegetarian and vegan supermarkets was assured. The success of this can be measured by the weekend queues for the tills. The food counter stocks vegan and vegetarian snacks and delicacies such as pâtés, marinated olives, cheeses, cakes and pastries. Elsewhere, there is a truly excellent range of health foods, wholefoods and organic produce, including some splendid wines, ciders and beers. The organic and seasonal produce might look like those on a Saturday evening game show of humorous vegetables with double entendre shapes, but they really do taste more complex. There is always a range of environmentally and ethically screened goods such as household cleaners and toiletries. Local suppliers are used where possible (herbs come from Glebelands in Sale) whilst a GM-free policy is maintained throughout. There are events, a good children's play area and toilets. In the quarterly newsletter, the price comparisons are fascinating. In August 2005, the British organic apples in Unicorn were £2.38 a kg. In Sainsburys, organic apples from New Zealand were £2.55 a kg. Sort of tells you something doesn't it.

Titanics

Waterloo Road, Cheetham Hill

0161 792 1888

www.titanics.co.uk

Winner of the 2005 Manchester Food and Drink Festival Best Retail Outlet and a real survivor - after 95 years of trade, is there an older deli in the North? It's a survivor in more ways than one. Founder Joseph Abraham Hyman was aboard the Titanic when it rendezvoused with an iceberg in 1912. His survival made him a local celebrity. After a spell in the States, he returned to Manchester where he became inevitably known as Mr Titanic. Inspired by the delis he had seen across the pond, Hyman decided to open a version in Manchester. The ship is steered today by Stanley Hyman and his son Richard, and under their navigation makes deliveries to Newcastle,

Bristol and Cardiff. An overachieving family, another Hyman is Clarissa, author of numerous Jewish cookery books including The Jewish Kitchen. The interior is a visual treat. This is the second site and there are lots of nostalgic artefacts from the first, demolished as part of a large-scale redevelopment, including rescued street signs such as Percival Street and Biscombe Street. Split into four distinct sections, there's a huge variety of kosher products ranging from wines and grape juices to meats including shin beef, pickled beef, chicken and a selection of 27 different varieties of sausages, all of which are prepared in the store. You'll also find herring preparations, including schmaltz herring, along with smoked salmon and hummus, matzos, olives, seeds and pates. Just don't ask for an iceberg lettuce...

Markets

Those in search of other good foodstuffs should visit the **Farmers Market** at Piccadilly Gardens (0161 234 7356 8D) in the city centre every second Friday and Saturday of the month. Here you will find a fantastic range of locally produced, good-quality, GM-free delights, including Lancashire honey, ostrich meat, wild boar, Cumberland sausages, free range lamb, geese, smoked trout, locally grown herbs, rhubarb, local cheeses and more. There's a constantly changing array of delights.

Look out for the **Christmas Market** in December and the **Food and Drink Festival Market** in October in the city centre. The first showcases European and seasonal produce, the second regional food and drink. They are variously located in Albert, St Ann's and Exchange Squares.

There are various local traditional food markets that occur in **Altrincham**, **Leigh**, **Ramsbottom**, **Saddleworth**, **Rochdale** and **Wigan** amongst others. But four are particularly worthy of a detour: Bolton, Bury, Stockport and Ashton. **Ashton** rs recovering from a fire last year and is held on the last Sunday of every month. Bolton (01204 336825) and Bury (0161 253 5111) really stand out - classic market halls filled with variety. They are always cheaper than big name supermarkets.

Bolton Market sells more than just scaly and slippery things, but the fish market is a wonder. Leave equipped with a five-star bargain bag of marvellous food and for a dose of pure theatre, visit on a Saturday from 2pm, when the stall-holders sell off their discounted fish calls.

Bury Market lies a short walk to the right of the Metrolink station entrance and attracts visitors from far and wide. The fish market is again excellent.

Stockport Market has an interesting site above the rest of the town, with a good Victorian market in the centre, but best of all on the south side there's a handsome Produce Hall, featuring, for example, Keith's Deli (0161 477 6333).

Local specialities

In Bury, a 20-minute tram ride north of the city, it's been going on commercially since at least 1818. You would kill the pig, collect the blood in a bucket and then roll your sleeve to the shoulder, stick your arm in to the elbow and stir. Pieces of fat were added and herbs for flavouring, and eventually you had **black pudding**. Bury market is still the place to get this delicacy: eaten fresh unaccompanied or with mustard, it is delicious.

Alongside black pudding, Lancastrians, especially in the former cotton producing districts around Manchester, would eat **cow heel pie**: steak and heel cooked together in gravy under a pastry topping or as a stew. Also popular was **rag pudding or beef roll**: minced steak, ham, breadcrumbs, anchovy sauce, flavourings, egg and milk bound inside a muslin cloth and boiled or steamed. You've probably heard of **Lancashire hotpot**: trimmed lamb chops, potatoes, onions, mushrooms, in layers, with trimmed lambs' kidneys as an optional extra. Not for the squeamish is **tripe**: the stomach lining of a cow, best eaten cold with plenty of vinegar. A more delicate dish was **emerald eggs**: fine-chopped parsley placed in the buttered cups of an egg poacher and the eggs turned out with the parsley on top. The inhabitants of our neighbour city Liverpool are even nicknamed after the local meat and veg stew, **scouse**. There are still several areas of Lancashire that retain traditional dishes with their colourful names intact, thus **slappy** (pie on a barmcake), **babbies yed** (meat pudding or pie), **slavvery duck**, **faggot**, **scraps** (fish batter and chips left in cooking fat/oil) and **pea wet** (pea juice, as in 'chips and pea wet').

Many dishes are seasonal. Traditionally, Christmas **mince**

continued page 156

Having survived aggressive competition from high street chains and supermarkets, the region's wine shops are well worth visiting. Especially as they can offer help and advice to both the novice and the experienced imbiber, which is lacking in, say, Tesco.

Portland Wine (0161 928 0357 www.portlandwine.co.uk) in Hale has an astute buying policy permitting them to offer many reasonably priced wines with an emphasis on rare and special. Sign up for the mailing list and you will receive a knowledgeable monthly update on latest offers. Twice a year on separate evenings, wide ranging Old and New World tasting events by the shop's suppliers are held at

extremely well stocked wine shop. Here you can spend anything from a fiver to a thousand quid. This wine utopia even extends to a tasting room complete with an inlaid tasting table, 24 custom-made chairs and, naturally, Reidel glasses.

Northeast of the city centre, Oldham is fortunate to possess **Winos** (0161 652 9396). For several years, ebullient owner Phil Garratt has imported wine from over the Channel and his shop is a tightly packed Aladdin's cave of interesting, good value wines. Garratt tries to taste everything he stocks and encourages his customers to do the same.

The city's two **Love Saves the Day** delis on Oldham Street (0161

With over 600 Spanish wines available in an area adjacent to a restaurant and for sale on or off the premises, it reminds people that Spain produces marvellous wines from many regions other than Rioja.

In Cathedral Street, **Harvey Nichols** (0161 828 8888 5B) has a small, superb range of wines, but they are expensive. Get on their mailing list, though, and you will be kept fully informed of prestigious wine events with food that are held periodically.

If you want to really treat yourself to a wine buff's dream, a short trip out to **D Byrne and Co** at New Market Street in Clitheroe (01200 442537) is highly recommended. Repeatedly voted the best regional

Wine shops

a nearby hotel. Though originally beer importers, **Carringtons** (0161 881 0099) in Chorlton have an impressive and keenly priced range. There are some Spanish rarities here and some excellent wines from Southern France. Port also features strongly. Now in its second year of trading in West Didsbury, **Reserve** (0161 438 0101 www.reservewines.co.uk) is the brainchild of ex-Oddbins employees Kate Chilton and Henry Boyes. Their infectious enthusiasm for wine is evident in the 400 different wines - most of them exclusive to the shop - and the way advice is given. Weekly tastings are held on Saturday afternoons. Nearby **Corks Out** (0161 881 9663 www.corksout.co.uk) on Princess Road is much bigger. For the past three years, former city centre sommeliers, Nathan and Craig, have assembled an eclectic choice of wines with a strong French emphasis. The shop is well known for champagnes and cavas.

Twenty miles northwest in the centre of Horwich, near Bolton, is **TH Wrights** (01204 697805) an

834 2266 9C) and Deansgate (0161 834 2266 www.lovesavesth eday.co.uk 3G) have strong wine slections. Champagne is a strong feature and membership of the wine club is recommended, with a long established tradition of outstanding tastings.

Evuna (0161 819 2752 4F) on Deansgate won the 2004 Best Wine List Award shortly after opening.

wine shop in the annual International Wine Challenge, it is a century-old family-run business with delightful cellars that run under the street. Claret is a strong point.

The success of the excellent Big Manchester Wine Tasting series of events during the Food and Drink Festival this year shows that the wine scene in Manchester gets bigger and bigger each year.

In September 2006, 300 anaesthetists attended a Flavour of the North West event in the Bridgewater Hall. At this point, most people ask if this is a joke, but no - it's serious. The sleepers were here on their national convention and they wanted their entertainment to refer directly to the place they'd chosen. Every bit of foodstuff, veg, meat, fish and fruit together with drinks such as beer, sarsaparilla,

medium-sized stores that have long shown a commitment to quality North Western food. They also sponsored the regional Food Producer of the Year Awards in 2005.

Aside from Booths it's best to seek out regional delights at the delis and Farmers Markets listed in this section, or in restaurants and pubs such as Sam's Chophouse, Le Mont, Obsidian, the Bridge, the River Restaurant,

Land of plenty

dandelion and burdock and so on, were sourced from within 50 miles of Manchester, from west of the Pennines and east of the Irish Sea. The anaesthetists were knocked out. That is a joke.

The reason for the range and excellence of the products is down to the North West itself, the most diverse region in the UK. From lowland Cheshire to the drained peat marshes of Lancashire, from Pennine moors to Lakeland mountains, from tidal estuaries to great cities, it is all here. Even the climate plays its part. A propensity for precipitation gives the North West the richest milk fields on the planet. That is why Cheshire man Lewis Carroll in *Alice in Wonderland* included that Cheshire cat with the cheesiest of grins. It was the cat that got the cream.

The bad news is that it's not so easy to access nature's bounty. This is the next step in the re-invention of top quality local food. At present the commitment of the major supermarkets to local producers merely amounts to tokenism. A very honourable exception in the North is Booths, the Lancashire-based chain of

Greens, Choice, Isinglass, Rhubarb, Marmalade and many other pubs and restaurants. A good one-stop shop is Northern Harvest (see column, right).

Celebrations to look out for include Manchester Food and Drink Festival in early October, the Nantwich International Cheese Festival in July, and the Food Lovers Festivals every year in Cumbria, Lancashire and Cheshire. For an idea of the range of North West produce and where to get it, contact North West Fine Foods (01695 732734 www.nwff.co.uk) - they also organise the Food Lovers Festivals.

This year's North West Producer of the Year Award went to Dew-Lay of Garstang for their Garstang Blue - handsomely pictured on this page. This is made using milk from a 15-mile radius of Dew-Lay's Garstang dairy. The runner-up - and favoured by several judges - was the pressed beef from Hartley's in Nelson, using the best silverside beef from Bowland Foods in Preston. One judge described it as 'a real original. Simple, robust and with great texture and taste and visual appeal - true to its area of origin'.

Doorstep farmer

Northern Harvest at Croft, near Warrington, delivers to a 30-mile radius, taking orders via the web, phone and fax. To read their catalogue is to drool, but also to learn how varied the food from the region can be. There are 2,000 products listed, including hams from the Cheshire Smokehouse, pork, lamb and beef from Bowland Outdoor Reared Meats, wild boar from Sillfield Farm, locally caught fish from Creative Seafoods, cheeses from Raven's Oak and ice cream from Tattenhall Dairy. Categories include baby foods, fruit and veg, oils, pulses, pâtés, pickles, ready-made meals, dried spices, beers, even fresh flowers. To make it a complete shop, there are some products that are not exclusively regional, such as olive oil and wine, but they all bear clear provenance. There's a small range of household goods too. Their seasonal hampers are a treat, £20-£150.
Northern Harvest, Kenyon Hall, Croft, Warrington (0845 6023309 www.northern harvest.co.uk).

The dilemma of British food

In 1769, a Manchester landlady, Elizabeth Raffald, wrote one of the first English cookbooks. It was called *The Experienced English Housekeeper*, ran to 13 editions and was pirated at least 23 times. It included recipes such as 'To make a Porcupine breast of veal' or 'To make moon and stars in jelly'. In 1773, she sold the copyright for the huge sum of £1,400.

Shortly after, the rot set in. To the Victorian middle classes, the indigenous cooking reminded them too much of their humble origins or of a querolous under class. It was shunted aside, in favour of all things Gallic: a classic case of too many parvenus with too many French fries on their shoulders. The prejudice continues today, fuelled by dietary fashions. Much British food was built for calorie collecting in order to survive in a cold climate. In our centrally heated existence, it's easier to get out the ciabatta and the sun-blushed tomatoes. Ludicrously, we ignore classic food combinations. No French restaurant would fail to offer regional wines. The best Manchester restaurants singularly fail to offer one of the excellent ales from the 14 independent breweries in the area. But a good ale is the perfect accompaniment for red meat dishes - easily as good as red wine.

A further problem is that to excel at British cooking takes care. We have an intricate cuisine pretending to be simple. Use of less than fresh ingredients, bad timing and any number of other potential hazards produces stodge. Gravy or pastry can come from hell or heaven.

Despite a recent surge of interest in traditional British cuisine, it remains in grave peril at family level, especially Lancashire and North-Western specialities. These were often the foods of the poor, foods that wasted nothing - similar indeed to that of many others such as Spanish and Chinese. As a child, my mother provided the following joys: full breakfasts, home-made bread, home-made soups, pies, stews, dumplings, spam fritters, fish, local vegetables, trifles, cakes, apple tarts, rhubarb tarts, ginger biscuits, oaties - the list goes on and on. On hot days, friends clamoured to come round for home-made lemonade. We had cheese on toast for supper or porridge with honey or syrup.

But it took forever to make and prepare. Modern lifestyles, with the necessity for both adult partners to work, preclude such regular home-made variety. It's difficult to envisage a renewal to the labour-intensive toil required in the British domestic kitchen. Increasingly, it's the responsibility of the professional chef to keep producing the best of traditional foods.

pies were prepared with minced beef, sweetened with dried fruit, raisins, sultanas and spices. On Bonfire Night, a typical speciality was **black peas**, soaked for 24 hours, boiled up and eaten with copious quantities of vinegar.

Mushy peas served locally in chip shops are a classic regional speciality. Untrustworthy Tykes claim that they invented **fish and chips**, but the first fish and chip shop in the country opened in 1863 in Mossley, 12 miles east of Manchester. Chips and, in some areas like Wigan even pies, are frequently served in barms or barmcakes, which the rest of the country calls bread rolls.

Lots of sweet stuff comes from the region, including **Eccles cakes** (raisins in sugary buns) and **Manchester tarts** (a pastry base with jam topped by custard - now becoming fashionable - and sometimes sprinkled with coconut). **Goosnargh cakes** are a sweet confection of butter, caraway seeds, flour and loaf sugar and should not be missed. **Bilberry tarts** made from moorland fruit are wonderful too, but for even greater sweetness try a stick of **Blackpool rock**. Equally tooth-rotting but far nicer are the boiled sweets, **Uncle Joe's Mintballs** from Wigan. **Love Hearts** come from New Mills on the edge of the conurbation.

The lush grass of the meadows encourages the ruminants to produce a creamy milk perfect for the delicious crumbly **Lancashire** and **Cheshire cheeses**. Local drinks abound too. Aside from ale (see the Pubs chapter), there is **Vimto** (the popular herbal drink now gone fizzy), **dandelion and burdock**; **sarsaparilla** (from the root of the same name) and **blackberry vinegar** (a medicinal warmer for winter). **Red Rose Whisky** from Wigan is the only English whisky and is as old as the Pennine Hills that supply its water.

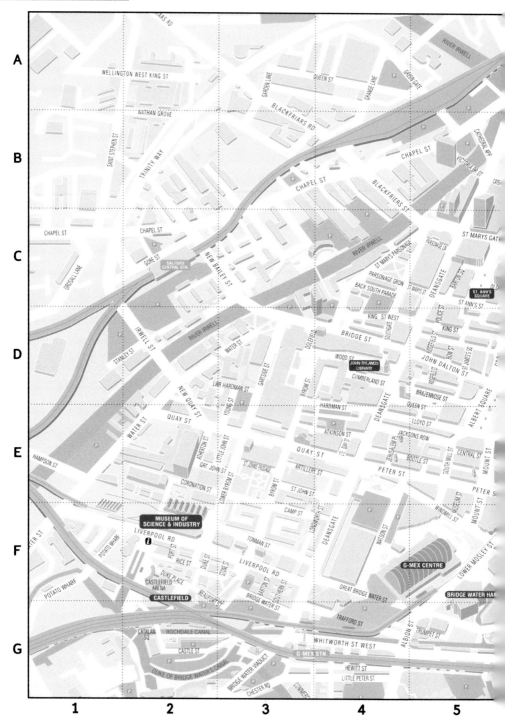

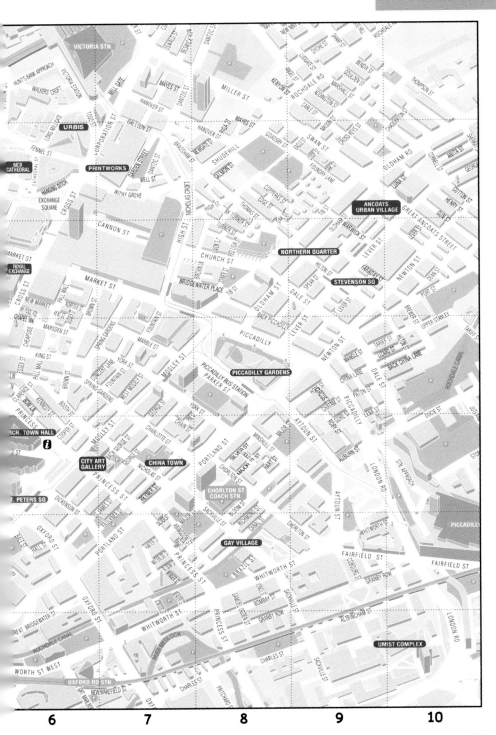

Map **161**